MARXIST LITERARY THEORY
and Reflections on Japanese Literature

MARXIST LITERARY THEORY
and Reflections on Japanese Literature

Wim Nuyten

iUniverse, Inc.
New York Lincoln Shanghai

MARXIST LITERARY THEORY
and Reflections on Japanese Literature

iUniverse books may be ordered through booksellers or by contacting:

iUniverse
2021 Pine Lake Road, Suite 100
Lincoln, NE 68512
www.iuniverse.com
1-800-Authors (1-800-288-4677)

ISBN-13: 978-0-595-40379-0 (pbk)
ISBN-13: 978-0-595-84754-9 (ebk)
ISBN-10: 0-595-40379-4 (pbk)
ISBN-10: 0-595-84754-4 (ebk)

Printed in the United States of America

Contents

Acknowledgements

I would like to express my sincere gratitude to Professor M. Sakabe and Professor Y. Ohashi, who gave their advice.

I am very grateful to Professor L. G. Perkins, who read all my writings and provided useful comments and advice.

Foreword

Twentieth century literary criticism is—there are exceptions—a definite hodge-podge of confusing, contradictory and invalid concepts of literary theory. Very often literary critics borrow concepts from various sciences such as linguistics, psychology, philosophy etc. Then, at random, they transplant these borrowed concepts into literary theory without having researched the functioning of these concepts in their original disciplines. For example the concept of 'signifier and signified' in linguistics has been appropriated by most literary critics as a basic tool for literary analysis. On closer examination, this concept turns out to be invalid, even for linguistics, which makes the scientific borrowing of this concept rejectable.

Twentieth century literary criticism has also been marked by a tendency to disconnect a text from its author and a tendency to destruct a text's intrinsic value on accord of the reader's free interpretation and use of a text. I stick to the conventional notion that author, text and reader, need each other and therefore oughtn't to be separated from each other. (Besides, every author is a reader, too.) Furthermore, author, text and reader, are born, exist and function at a certain time in a specific society; elements such as time, society, and their respective changes have to be included in a realistic literary theory.

For the foregoing reasons I don't depart from established literary theories to obtain a better understanding of Japanese literature. In Part 1, I depart from the common sense of a dictionary's definition of literature. Drawing upon this defini-tion, I develop and give concrete embodiment to this definition and consequently I extract a number of mechanisms that are at work in literature and its produc-tion against the background of present-day society. I test and evaluate these mechanisms by analysing mainly Japanese literature. Finally, I bring literature and literary production back into contact with society.

In Part 2, I review and comment—with additional quotations from Japanese literature—on linguistic concepts from F. de Saussure, and the literary concepts from V. Shklovsky, R. Jakobson, R. Barthes (all three are representatives of struc-turalism) and the literary concepts from J. Lacan, J. Derrida and M. Fouault (the last three being representatives of post-structuralism). This overview doesn't include the literary philosophy of M. Bakhtin because he doesn't really fit into one stream of literary theory. Bakhtin is often wrongly described as a Marxist critic although he never refers to Marx nor does he incorporate basic Marxist concepts into his literary theory. Bakhtin's insights and concepts are nevertheless so unique that I describe part of his literary theories in a separate chapter.

In chapter 3, Part 2, I quote Saikaku's short story *Everlasting Edo Stores* (1691). Starting from the original printed version, I fully use my multi-language consciousness to provide a modern Japanese version and an English translation, which is followed with an analysis. This chapter mainly confirms most of the mechanisms that are at work in literature and literary production, which were found in Part 1. I test the theses and concepts of literary theory which I develop while reviewing and comenting on the foregoing mentioned critics in the context of my short story "The Woman in the Red Coat" (chapter 4, Part 2).

Part 3 deals solely with Marxist criticism. Marxism's impact on the organisation of the international labor movement; its impact on world history: the Russian, the Chinese and Cuban revolutions; Marxism's influence on the social sciences: mainly sociology, historiography and economics; Marxism's indirect influence on philosophy, linguistics and anthropology: this all makes it evident that Marxism deserves careful consideration in this study of literary theory. In the first chapter of Part 3, I give an overview of Marx's and Engels' ideas about literature, while contrasting their ideas with Lenin's and Trotsky's ideas and, I reach the following conclusion:

To avoid misunderstandings I think that it's necessary to limit the use of 'Marxist'—'Marxism' to only Marx's and Engels' theories! Marxism's deviants such as Leninism, Stalinism and Trotskyism and their originators ought to be kept separate from the human and critical Marxism which was developed by Marx and Engels.

In the second chapter of Part 3, I draw up three Marxist theses for literary theory. I also develop three Marxist criteria to distinguish classes because 'class' and 'class struggle' are central concepts of Marxist Theory; though I have to acknowledge these concepts lesser usefulness for literary theory. I briefly cover the faulty theories of present-day Marxist critics as well. Finally, I apply the Marxist theses for literary theory in analysing O. Dazai's novel *The Setting Sun* which brings forth a fourth Marxist thesis for literary theory.

Appendix A contains my short story *Interview with Karl Marx: Engelsism*, which I wrote under the nom de plume of Alexander Huysmans. This short story's advantage over an academic description of Marxism are manifold: we get to know K. Marx from his bourgeois family and educational background. The story clears up the existing misconceptions about communism and Marxism; the story clarifies the private and historical circumstances under which Marx and his friend F. Engels had to develop their political activities and their political and economical writings. At this place it's worthwile to dwell on the opinion of the Marxist critic G. Lukács (1885–1971) regarding the necessity of a **scientific** auto-biography when writing about great historical figures: 'It is quite understandable that the liberated mass of workers in the Soviet Union should wish for lively, comprehensible and moving accounts of the lives of their loved and revered lead-ers Marx and Engels, Lenin and Stalin. These wishes can and must be satis-fied...by scientific biographies on a high literary level...' (*The Historical Novel*)

G. Lukács stresses: 'all the individual features of Marx and authentic quota-tions from Marx's texts can not appear convincing in a literary adaption: in their original context they are both more powerful in themselves as well as more humanly immediate than they could possibly be in any such literary adaption.' These quotations evince why I can't consider G. Lukács as a Marxist critic: it's outrageous to write about 'the liberated mass of workers in the Soviet Union' of 1937, while at that time, too, everybody was well aware of Stalin's repressive dic-tatorship. How could G. Lukács mention Stalin, in one breath with Marx and Engels, as a revered leader? Marx and Engels who wanted to 'create' a society where free individual development should have to be the condition for everyone's development; a society that would be so far apart from Stalin's Soviet Union!

Marx's and Engels' traditional and open-minded ideas about literature give me enough leeway to reject Lukács' preference for a scientific autobiography over a literary story. For scientific purpose we can study Marx's and Engels' theories in their publications; their collected works provide more than enough autobio-graphical information about Marx and Engels, too; what remains to be done is to humanize Marx and Engels; to bring out their beauty and ugliness, their strength and weakness; to reproduce their life and work on a different-higher-level.

Appendix B is my account of the Japanese philosopher T. Watsuji's book *Cli-mate*. This account **isn't related** to literary theory but it's instructive to under-stand the present-day Japanese society in which Japanese teachers, TV programmes, newspapers, politicians etc. keep spreading 'propaganda' about the uniqueness and specialness of the Japanese race and its culture. Many of these ideas about Japaneseness come directly from the nationalist philosopher T. Wat-suji and his book *Climate*.

PART 1

LITERATURE FRAMED WITHIN SOCIETY

1

Some Elementary Introductory Remarks

A Definition of literature:

Writings in prose or verse, especially writings having excellence of form or expression and expressing ideas of permanent or universal interest. The production of literary work especially as an occupation. [1]

This quoted definition emphasizes the content side of literature and describes producing literature as an occupational activity. The definition has one shortcoming: not properly considering the consuming side of literary production. I propose to remedy this shortcoming by inserting the words '*and the reading thereof*' in the definition. Literature: writings in prose or verse, and the reading thereof, especially writings having excellence of form or expression and expressing ideas of permanent or universal interest. The production of literary works especially as an occupation.

Looking at literature from the production side, we observe that thoughts, feelings, impressions in the writer's mind, echoes that emanate from his or her life, are processed into literature. This concept of being 'processed' is the key to understanding mechanisms at work in the literary consumption-production process.

Every writer lives in a society that feeds him or her in a material and non-material way. In turn, the writer gives material and non-material feedback to society. It's important to reflect on the order: first, the writer is fed by—consumes—from society, before he or she, by way of his or her literary production, returns his or her feedback to society.

The writer is born and develops himself or herself, in an existing, functioning society. Language knowledge is the main component required to develop an individual into a writer. Before an individual starts to produce literature, he or she has consumed a certain amount of language (spoken–written–sung–heard—read), fixed language patterns, meanings and functions. Language consumption takes place in the family, at school, in a bar, in prison, in church: in society. This consumption may occur in a natural way, such as a baby listening to new sounds or from curiosity when a child or adult reads books searching for knowledge.

Nowadays a large amount of consumption is obligatory; compulsory at schools, universities and places of employment. In present-day society, the Ministry of Education, the newspaper company board of directors, broadcasting corporations, prison authorities, decide and establish, to a large extent, what language in general, and which literature in particular, their students, readers, watchers and inmates are allowed to consume.

Language functions of speech, writing, singing, hearing and reading, can change from one moment being consumptive to another moment being productive. These language functions form a unity in variety, considered from the literary production perspective. These language functions are fused into an organic literary work through the writer.

The consumptive-productive natures in the language function of reading. Many people read the Bible (one of the oldest and most widely read books) without posing any questions during this consumptive process. One might wonder about the origin of this book; the divergency in theological meanings that are caused by translating original Bible manuscripts from Hebrew into Greek, Latin, and later into other languages; the logic and contradictions in various parts of the Bible as it was written by different authors. Yet, millions of readers have ignored these problems and just have 'absorbed' the biblical text.

Perhaps they read the Bible as they would read a detective novel; for pure, passive reading pleasure. The same holds true for the majority of Charles Dickens' contemporary readers. They consumed his novels, such as *Oliver Twist* and *David Copperfield*, which exposed the evils of their society, without any drastic change in their thinking and behavior. These readers were engaged in a passive consumptive reading process.

In the case of productive reading, I'm thinking about the Bible read by F. Engels when he was eighteen. In several of Engels' letters to his school friend F. Graeber, he writes about the contradictions and different interpretations that crosses his mind while 'consuming' the Bible.

> *There are some quite obvious contradictions in the Bible. How can you square the two genealogies of Joseph, Mary's husband, the different accounts of the institution of the Eucharist ("this is my blood"; this is the new testament in my blood...The*

statement that the mother of Jesus went out to look for her son, whom she believed to be mad, although she had conceived him miraculously...Where does the Bible demand literal belief in its teachings, in its accounts?

F. Engels didn't read the Bible for pure, passive reading pleasure, but with a deep, active interest. One might wonder where and when does Engels' consumptive reading of the Bible change into productive reading? Language functions such as reading and writing aren't bluntly opposed to each other. The same holds true for the relation between consumptive and productive natures of reading: these natures influence and run over into each other. The following quotation perfectly reflects this process of running over into each other; Engels writes:

> *And yet it is written; "Seek, and ye shall find. Or what man is there of you, whom if his son ask bread, will give him a stone?...how much more shall your Father which is in Heaven?" Tears come into my eyes as I write this. I am moved to the core, but I feel I shall not be lost; I shall come to God, for whom my whole heart yearns.*[3]

To uncover the productive reading's nature, I propose the following intervention: *Tears come into my eyes as* **I read, think, reflect and write this.** Engels' reading and writing activities entered into a relationship; they influenced and started running over into each other. This originating directly from the **reading** activity **'think–reflect–write–process'**, I call productive reading.

I stated in the beginning of this chapter: 'before an individual starts to produce literature, he or she, has consumed a certain amount of language (spoken–written–sung–heard–read), fixed language patterns, meanings and language functions.' However, anyone who writes (letters, essays, stories), can't be qualified as a participant of—contributor to—literary production. We need to expand a little further on the occupational aspect of literary production. Generally speaking, everybody needs to provide his subsistence by working. Publishers, booksellers, printers and writers are subjected to the market-mechanism of capitalism while being involved in the production of literature. Literature may be produced, printed and published, but if it doesn't turn out a profit, the writer's livelihood and with him the livelihood of thousands of other people are risked. The supply side of the market (production and sales) is influenced by economical forces: in the final analysis, literature must be a profitable product. Even when a rich writer doesn't have to earn his or her living from his or her writings; all the others involved (printers, publishers etc.,) want to—and have to—make money out of the literary production business.

Before we look closer at the literary production of Yasunari Kawabata, a Japanese Nobel Prize winning novelist, I want to stress once more the importance of the relationship between consumptive and productive natures of various language functions. A writer who starts literary production, remains at the same time a consumer of language. His literary production will reflect his—almost—predetermined language consumption. That's why a literary product can't be something completely new or unique. Only when a writer can process all his thoughts, feelings, impressions etc. in a unique form, expresses ideas of permanent or universal interest, provides artistic joy to humankind for centuries; only then can we use the term literary production.

To summarize provisionally what has been said so far:

1. The writer processes his or her thoughts, feelings, impressions, echoes emanating from his or her life in a functioning society into a literary product.

2. The writer's main tool 'language knowledge' has been largely set and predetermined.

3. Language functions have a consumptive and a productive nature, which may interrelate, influence and run over into each other.

4. Language functions form a unity in variety that through the writer are fused into an organic literary product.

5. Literary production is subjected to the market mechanisms of present capitalist society; it has to turn out a profit.

6. A literary product can't be something completely new or unique, although processed through the writer in a unique form or style, expressing ideas of permanent or universal interest, it may provide artistic joy to mankind for centuries.

NOTES

1. Webster Third New International Dictionary, unabridged, Merriam-Webster U. S. A., 1961.

2. Karl Marx/ Frederick Engels, Collected Works, Volume 2, New York, International Publishers, Copyright Progress Publishers, Moscow, 1975, p. 426

3. Ibid., p. 461.

2

Yasunari Kawabata

The Japanese writer Y. Kawabata (1899–1972), had a very lonely childhood. Born as the son of a physician in Osaka, he had one sister, Yoshiko, who was seven years older. His father had a frail health and died one year after Kawabata's birth. After his father's death, Kawabata moved to his mother's home, but when he was three years old, his mother died of tuberculosis and Kawabata moved in with his father's parents. At the age of eight he lost his older sister. From then on he only lived with his grandfather, who became blind when Kawabata was fourteen. Kawabata nursed his grandfather for two years till his grandfather died. During this period he wrote *The Diary of a Sixteen-Year-Old* which was published in the literary magazine *Bungeijidai* in the 1925 August and September issues (ten years after his grandfather's death). We can divide *The Diary's* [1] contents into eight categories: 1. the progress of his grandfather's illness, 2. grandfather's spoken words, 3. grandfather's feelings, 4. grandfather's actions, 5. Yasunari's school life, 6. Yasunari's spoken words, 7. Yasunari's feelings and 8. Yasunari's actions. The various thoughts, feelings, impressions and echoes that emanate from Yasunari's life and environment are processed into his diary. In the above order of categories I will take some excerpts from the *Diary of a Sixteen-Year-Old* that exemplify these categories.

1. *'Grandfather probably foresees his own death.'*

2. *'I'm not in the least attached to life in this world.'*

3. *'Our family has descended from Yasutoki Hojo and we have continued for seven hundred years. I hope he will succeed our family as usual. Our family should quickly return to prosperous times.'*

4. *'Oh, is that so? Ha, ha, ha, ha, ha,'* he laughed in a sad voice.

5. *'School is my paradise.'*

6. *'To decide man's course for his lifetime is difficult,' said grandfather suddenly, in a deep tone. 'Yes, it's difficult,' I answered.*

7. *I finished my meal, rolled up my sick grandfather's mattress and took the chamber-pot.*

8. *If I can continue writing a hundred pages in my diary, grandfather might be saved.*

By writing this diary—and in spite of the polishing while rewriting the diary for publication—the writer informs us of his thoughts and feelings that arose when taking care of his grandfather. Kawabata's feelings of affection, hate, loneliness etc. are compounded in the writing process.

At the age of eighteen Kawabata already expressed his aspiration to become a writer: 'As all other young people have to follow their course in life, I am in the same dreadful position. Therefore, the urge to publish my writings stirs my emotions.'[2] At this young age, Kawabata published eight stories in newspapers and magazines. However he soon stopped contributing his literary work for publication because: 'I became ashamed of the shallowness of my ideas; I also lost interest in the vulgar newspaper, and besides the person who used to be in charge had been replaced.'[3]

In 1917, Kawabata moved to Tokyo, where he first enrolled in a preparatory school and in September that year, he began his studies in the Faculty of English Literature at Daiichi Higher School. The next year Kawabata went on his first trip to Izu Peninsula in Shizuoka Prefecture, where he met and befriended a troupe of strolling entertainers with whom he travelled along. In 1920, Kawabata enrolled in the Faculty of English Literature at Tokyo Imperial University, where the next year he changed to the Faculty of Japanese Literature. During his student years Kawabata published about thirteen short stories in various literary magazines.

The Izu Dancer (Izu no Odoriko). The publication of *The Izu Dancer* made Kawabata famous. This literary work was based on two important events in Kawabata's life. The first event was his trip to Izu Peninsula in 1918, where he befriended the troupe of strolling entertainers. The second event was his marriage proposal, to sixteen-year-old Michiko, which she accepted. However, while Kawabata was making wedding preparations in Tokyo, he received a letter from Michiko, who stayed in Gifu Prefecture, in which she rejected the wedding proposal. This must have been a very bitter experience for Kawabata who was imbued with the spirit of love and marriage.

Half a year after this shocking experience, Kawabata wrote the manuscript *Memories of Yugashima* while he stayed at the Yumoto Inn in Yugashima City in 1922. The first part from this unfinished manuscript consisted of material for *The Izu Dancer* and Kawabata used the second part to write *Boy* (*Shonen*), which he completed in 1948. When he finished this story Kawabata destroyed the original manuscript.

The concept of *The Izu Dancer*. A fitting method of reviewing *The Izu Dancer* is to study a number of passages.[4]

> *I was twenty years old; I wore the Higher School's cap, a dark blue kimono and a book sack over my shoulder.*

This sentence projects Kawabata himself as the leading character in the beginning of this story. In the sentences that precede and follow the above quoted sentence, Kawabata describes, in a very rich, creative way the scenery and weather. In describing the scenery, the places he had stayed etc., there is a sentence in the middle of this first page that expresses the student's—Kawabata's—mental state: 'Excited by a certain hope, I hurried along the road.' True to his expectation, when the student reaches the tea-house, he meets the troupe of strolling entertainers for the third time: 'The little dancing girl saw me standing and quickly turned over the cushion she had been sitting on and pushed it toward me.'

Without being asked or ordered, the little dancing girl quickly gave her cushion to the student. Does this action express her feeling for the student? The student—Kawabata—interprets her action this way, but I would like to add a different interpretation. The little dancing girl, conditioned by her culture and social position, was brought up as a strolling entertainer with the purpose of serving customers. The little dancing girl's activities, such as singing, dancing, offering liquor, beating the drum, handing an ashtray to customers, playing the 'shamisen' (a Japanese three-stringed guitar); are based on her upbringing and culture. The girl's motivation to automatically give her cushion to the student can not be explained only by her feelings for him.

After the troupe of strolling entertainers left the tea-house, the student engages in a conversation with the old woman who keeps the tea-house:

'Where will the strolling entertainers stay tonight?' 'People like that; how to tell where they will stay, mister. Where ever they can find customers they will stay. They haven't the slightest idea which inn it will be tonight, do they?' The old woman's words filled with deep contempt stirred my emotions, because, then, I imagined letting the little dancing girl stay in my room tonight.

The student speaks about the strolling entertainers in usual, polite language but the old woman, in contrast uses words of contempt. She calls the strolling entertainers, 'People like that'. She addresses the student as 'mister' (or master). In short, Kawabata fixed his characters' social position by language: the language content and the degree of politeness expressed by the characters' speeches in regard to each other.

With a gap of four years, Kawabata processed his thoughts, feelings and echoes that emanated from his life and from his surrounding society into a literary work. The language function of listening was dormant for four years. Kawabata thought, felt and reflected about the old woman's words four years later when he was writing his manuscript. At the time of writing, his consumptive listening changed into productive listening. This productive nature of listening isn't made obvious only by the process of writing, but also in the stirring up of the student's—writer's—emotions and imagination to such an extent that Kawabata was inspired to base his literary production on words he had heard four years before.

On the road from Amagi Pass to Yugano, the student catches up with the troupe of strolling entertainers, engages in conversation with them and is accepted as their travel companion. Arriving in Yugano, they rest for one hour together in a cheap lodging house, after which the man of the troupe (the troupe consisted of one man, three women and a girl), takes the student to a hot-spring inn where the student lodges separately from the troupe. That evening the troupe is called to a party in a restaurant across from their inn. From his hotel the student hears the party's laughter, banter and music. Listening to the party the student feels and thinks as follows:

'Ah, the little dancing girl is still at the party. She is still sitting and playing the drum.' It was intolerable for me when the drum beating stopped. I felt as if I were being drowned by the sound of the rain. Soon everybody was chasing each other or dancing; the sound of a confusion of footsteps continued for a while. And then, complete silence returned. I kept a watchful eye. I tried to glare through the darkness to find out what was happing during the silence. I worried whether the little dancing girl would be having sex with someone tonight.

This is one of the most attractive passages from *The Izu Dancer*. The sound of the drum beat gives the student inner-peace, but the student is overwhelmed by uneasiness when the silence falls. The student's uneasiness is caused by his passion for the little dancing girl who might have sex with someone else. The silence after the drum beat stops or expressed differently, the little dancing girl's silence is contrasted with the sound of the rain. This contrast is intermingled with the student's desperate, perplexed, emotional feelings. The various sounds of footsteps, the drum beat, the rain, contrast with silence: the sense of hearing being contrasted with the sense of seeing—or in this case not seeing. These contrasts arouse two feelings in the student: 1. the little dancing girl stirs up his passion, and 2. his desperate, perplexed feeling that the object of his passion, the little dancing girl, might have sex with someone else. The tension between these two feelings is already destroyed in the middle of the story. It's the scene where the student sees the little dancing girl running out of a public bath. That moment he realizes that the object of his passion isn't a mature woman but 'she was a child, a mere child'. From this scene onwards, the story's theme changes to the student's psychological struggle to overcome his feelings of loneliness and the desire to be accepted by people as their friend. In the story 'Boy' Kawabata explains about this struggle: 'Brought up in unfortunate, unnatural circumstances, I had become a stiff, distorted person. People's kindness towards me felt like a personal blessing.'

The student's feeling of love for the little dancing girl is converted into the expectation of being accepted by other people (for example the troupe of strolling entertainers). On the way from Yugano to Shimoda, the student walks with the man of the troupe about eight or nine meters ahead of the women. Then the student hears the women talking about him:

> *'He's a good person, isn't he?'* [the little dancing girl said]
> *'Well, he seems to be good.'* [one of the women answers]
> *'He really is a good person. I like having someone so good.'* [the little dancing girl said]

Hearing this conversation about him, the student—Kawabata—was swayed by various emotions and a new way of looking upon his own life crossed his mind. The overheard conversation influenced Kawabata emotionally—he reflected about the conversation—and he wrote the conversation down. He consumed language to produce his literary work.

Near the end of the story, the student stays his last night of the trip in an inn run by the ex-mayor of Shimoda. The troupe of strolling entertainers stays in the

Koshuya, a cheap lodging-house. The themes of unattainable love (passion), feeling of loneliness and the difference in social position, are once more reinforced when the student isn't allowed to take the little dancing girl to the cinema. After going alone to the cinema, he comes back in his room and stares at Shimoda. He observes: 'The town was dark. I thought of hearing the unending sound of the drum beat. For no good reason I found myself weeping.' The previously hurting loneliness is now changed into an accepted loneliness. The next morning, the student says farewell to the little dancing girl and her brother (the man of the troupe) at the pier in Shimoda and boards the boat to Tokyo.

In the last passage of the story, the student weeps again, but this time it's a joyful, liberating weeping: 'I wept freely. It was as though my head had turned into clear water. The tears kept on streaming down. After that nothing remained but a generous, pleasant feeling.'

In the previous chapter I stated that language functions can change from one moment being consumptive to another moment being productive. The way *The Izu Dancer* was produced is a fitting example of this theory.

Language consumption   During the trip in Izu Peninsula

⇓

Literary production   *Memories of Yugashima*

⇓

Literary consumption   'Plundered' the unpublished manuscript 'Memories of Yugashima'

⇓

Literary production   *The Izu Dancer*

Redefinitions. In my reflections on Japanese literature I started from the writer's (Kawabata's) life after which I shifted my attention to his literary product *The Izu Dancer*. Using this approach, I've gained the insight that my previous observation (1. the writer processes his or her thoughts, feelings…2. the writer's main tool 'language knowledge" has benn…etc.) needs to be redefined.

We have seen that the little dancing girl might have behaved friendly towards the student for three reasons:

1. She likes the student. (This is Kawabata's interpretation.) 2. She is conditioned by her upbringing, social position and culture, to serve customers. (This is my interpretation.) 3. A combination of these reasons. This leads to redefining

my first observation: The writer **consciously, subconsciously and unconsciously** processes his thoughts, feelings, impressions, echoes, emanating from his life in a functioning society, into a literary product.

This redefinition creates two new theses about mechanisms that are at work in literary production and literature.

7. A writer brings unintentional meanings, motives and understandings into his or her literary work.

8. From different viewpoints—psychological, social-political, historical etc.—we can establish different interpretations of a literary work.

NOTES

1. The quoted passages from *Ju-Roku Sai no Nikki*, (*The Diary of a Sixteen-Year-Old*), are from: Yasunari Kawabata, Collected Works I, *Ju-Roku Sai no Nikki*, (*The Diary of a Sixteen-Year-Old*), Tokyo, Shueisha, 1972, pp. 115-131. Translated by W. Nuyten.

2. Ibid., p. 413.

3. Ibid., p. 416.

4. The quoted passages from *The Izu Dancer*, (*Izu no Odoriko*), are from; Yasunari Kawabata, Collected Works I, *Izu no Odoriko*, (*The Izu Dancer*), Tokyo, Shueisha, 1972, pp. 95-114. Translated by W. Nuyten.

3

Villon's Wife—Various Viewpoints

When I started to explore *The Izu Dancer*, I first gave a brief autobiographical sketch of Kawabata's lonely, sad youth. I will start the next exploration from the literary work itself and later make the connection with the writer and his life.

The title *Villon's Wife*[1] is very exotic. In the Japanese language 'Villon' is written in 'Katakana'—the square Japanese syllabary mainly used in writing foreign names and words—and 'Wife' ('tsuma') is written in the Chinese ideographic script called 'Kanji' which was adopted by the Japanese in the third century. This combination of a foreign word 'Villon' with the Japanese word 'tsuma' produces the effect of tension between the unknown and the already known word. Possibly I was lured to read this story because of the title's exotic appeal. At the beginning of the story, it's clear that a woman, who has a two or three-year old son, is the leading character and narrator. Without ever being addressed by her real name, she is called 'wife', waitress', 'Tsubaki's (a bar name) Sachan, etc. I will call this narrator 'missis'.

***Villon's Wife's* opening sentence:** 'Hurriedly, the noise of the front-door opening could be heard. I woke up because of this noise; that was, as usual, my dead drunken husband coming home at midnight, so I stayed silenty in bed.'

What kind of thoughts, feelings etc. are processed in this sentence? Without overinterpreting I will infer some referential meanings[a] from the passage and then consider them from various points of view. I will use 'historical', 'different language' and 'style' viewpoints to get a better picture of the information processed in the opening sentence. I chose the historical viewpoint to explore society's fast changing standards. The different language viewpoint is important to verify the practicality of translating, and the style viewpoint brings out a writer's technique.

Let's return to the opening sentence and its referential meanings:

1. The passage describes a couple's life. 2. Missis doesn't use her husband's name. 3. They are living in a small house. 4. The husband has the habit of drinking and coming home late. 5. Missis has a self-possessed character. 6. The husband is in a hurry. 7. Missis didn't stay up for her husband coming home.

Historical Viewpoint. What social position does this couple occupy in society? From the commentary I know that the story was published in 1947 and the story's contents are related to the period 1944–1946, just around the end of the Second World War.

The Japanese Civil Law from 1896 stipulated that a marriage should be effected by registration into the family register.[2] However, according to ancient Japanese tradition; if a couple performed a wedding ceremony and then started living together, they were considered by society as married.[3] Till the amendment to the Civil Code (1947) the position of Japanese women was inferior to that of Japanese men. For example, the wife could be found guilty of adultery but the husband could not.

---

[a] I define a referential meaning as one of the many possible meanings that can be inferred from the text in relation to its context and society.

The Civil Code of 1896 and 1898 favored the paternal family system. Professor H. Tanaka gives the following explanation:

> There were a great number of cases where the registration of the marriage was deliberately withheld by the defacto husband until he and/or his parents found the defacto wife acceptable or until the first baby was born of the defacto marriage. Thus, as a matter of fact, the Civil Code ironically sanctioned a sort of trial marriage and strengthened the paternal family system.[4]

The post-war New Japanese Constitution, a legacy of the American Occupation, gave women—twenty years after universal male suffrage—the right to vote in 1947. From a social and legal viewpoint, the meaning of marriage in 1945 differs from the present-day meaning. Missis, being in an inferior postion to her husband, might prefer using the detached 'husband' instead of the more intimate choice of his first name.

That the couple lives in a small house can be deduced from the fact that missis wakes up because of the noise of the front-door opening. In a large house where the front door is separated by a hall and corridors from the living and bedrooms, a sleeping person is rarely awakened by the sound of a front-door being opened. Referential meanings 4., 5., 6., and 7. are, from a historical viewpoint, very common. These situations could be encountered from ancient times up to the present, throughout the world. When taking social, religious, or psychological viewpoints to understand these meanings, we face a new challenge.

Considering the poverty of the period 1944–1946, the husband's drinking habit must be a heavy financial burden on a usual family. This leaves three possible explanations: 1. the husband is from a wealthy family, 2. the husband is an alcoholic, and 3. a combination of these explanations. When we read the complete story; will this straightforward interpretation prove right? What can we learn if we compare this story's 'alcoholic' husband with another famous alcoholic character? Let us for example consider Marmeladov, a character in Dostoyevsky's novel *Crime and Punishment*. Although Marmeladov is out of work—he had previously been a civil servant—and his wife and children are starving at home; Marmeladov asks his daughter Sonya, who works as a prostitute to support her family, for money to drink. One day, when Marmeladov is getting drunk, he meets the former college student Raskolnikov. **The fate** of this degenerating Marmeladov, the murder-committing Raskolnikov and Sonya, who sacrifies herself for both her father and Raskolnikov, **cuts through all layers of society.** Dostoyevsky's characters are the products of a Russian society in which the feudal system is breaking down; a society in change!

The background of *Villon's Wife* is a highly stratified Japanese society in 1946, because—as we later will see—the husband's unusual behavior doesn't influence or change his position in society. The highly stratified Japanese society in 1946, didn't create the necessary space for an aristocrat's [b] downfall.

How is missis' self-possessed character related to the institution of marriage? How does the institution of marriage function? First, we will have to define 'marriage. The key-word for marriage in Japan is 'join together ('musubi-tsukeru'). From long ago this word conveyed the meaning of marriage. In ancient times the God of marriage was called 'Musubi no Kami': 'Musubi' means childbirth and 'Kami' stands for the spirit of creating heaven and earth. In other words, the God of marriage is the spiritual force that makes the bond between man and woman.

---

[b] The writer Osamu Dazai—like his character 'the husband—was the son of one of the wealthiest landowners in Aomori Prefecture; his father served in both the Lower House and the House of Peers.

The second part of the key-word 'join together', in Japanese 'tsukeru', stands for producing (crops, finance), having sexual intercourse etc. Concludingly, the essence of marriage is based on the spiritual force that unites man and woman to produce, to have sexual intercourse and give childbirth.

What's the essence of marriage in the West compared with ancient Japan? For example from ancient Greece, we have Demosthenes' (384–322 B.C.) aphorism about marriage: 'Mistresses we keep for the sake of pleasure, concubines for the daily care of our persons, but wives to bear us legitimate children and to be faithful guardians of our households.'[5] This aphorism stresses the birth of legitimate descendants to protect a household and its property. For the male in ancient Greece, sex was not strictly limited to marriage. Though for married women, sex and marriage were fixed in a tightly knit form.

From ancient times up through the Middle Ages, individual sex love existed only among the slaves; the new arising class of free citizens made sex love by adultery because marriage itself was still decided by family interests and not by individual preferences:

> *Together with the Industrial Revolution (18th and 19th centuries), especially in Protestant countries…marriage remained class marriage, but, within the confines of the class, the parties were accorded a certain degree of freedom to choose…. In short, love marriage was proclaimed a human right…. this human right differed from all other so-called human rights. While, in practice, the latter remained limited to the ruling class, the bourgeoisie—the oppressed class, the proletariat, being directly or indirectly deprived of them—the irony of history asserts itself again. The ruling class continues to be dominated by well-known economic influences and, therefore, only in exceptional cases does it bear witness to really voluntary marriages; whereas, as we have seen, these are the rule among the dominated class.* [6] *(F. Engels)*

Freedom of choice, which allows sexual love, has entered the institution of marriage although it's still restricted to partners of the same class; mainly the proletariat. For the bourgeoisie, Engels observes that marriage remains dominated by the familiar economic influences. Considering Demosthenes' aphorism again; it wasn't his purpose to divide a man's life into three spheres. Demosthenes used this aphorism in a moral dispute when a charge was brought against the child from a prostitute, who wasn't an Athenean citizen. His aphorism aims to designate legitimate children and property as the basic elements of marriage.

How did the institution of marriage in Japan develop? The conclusion of a marriage depended on the agreement of the couple themselves, their parents and society as we can learn from the following observation:

> [from the Middle Ages] *the most important feature of the marriage ceremony was the exchange of nuptial cups at the bride's home, followed by the exchange of nuptial cups at the groom's home.... Then, the bride and groom ate and drank with the village people to receive their consent.* [the same source about marriage and virginity] *Virginity is respected after Confucian morals spread among the masses since Meiji era (1866–1912). Before that, virginity was even detested.* [7]

The previously used key-word 'join together' and my description of the essence of marriage in ancient Japan, lacked the agreement of parents, the couple themselves and society; it didn't include the disregard for virginity of the marriage partners.

From the sixteenth century (Early Modern Japan), a married couple in Japan is a unit that shares the burden of social and financial responsibility. This explains the Japanese custom of adopting a son, a son-in-law, or a young girl—when there are no sons or only unsuitable sons—to continue the household, including its social and economical position.

In *Villon's Wife*, missis' self possessed character can be explained from the preceding information. She only shares the social and financial responsibility of marriage with her husband. Matters like adultery committed by the husband or his coming home drunk late at night, don't influence the preservation of their marriage. From the beginning of their marriage, the element of free sex love based on personal beauty, close intimacy, similarity of tastes, respect for virginity (before marriage), isn't necessarily lacking but it's not the foundation of their marriage.

A Different Language Viewpoint. I will give the literal translation from the openings passage of 'Villon's Wife':

> '*Hurriedly hall opening sound can be heard, I because of this sound, woke up, but, that's my drunken husband's late at night's coming home be sure as to be as, in that condition silently was sleeping.*'

This word-for-word translation, although very awkward to read, shows us that in the original Japanese text the subject 'I' appears only once while in the English translation it appears twice. Very often the subject is omitted in Japanese: it can be deduced from the context. In spite of making a word-for-word translation, I can't convey the differences between common and polite Japanese. The English 'to be' can be translated from the common Japanese 'desu' or from the polite form 'gozaru'. The subject 'I' can be rendered into sixteen different Japanese words; polite, less polite, commmon, vulgar, female, male, etc. In *Villon's Wife,* missis uses the polite forms of 'I' and 'to be' which indicates her refined character. Japanese language creates various meanings by its rich vocabulary, but these Japanese meanings are dissolved in an English translation.

On the other hand, Japanese language doesn't distinguish[c] between singular and plural forms, masculine-feminine and neuter gender of nouns, adjectives and pronouns. Frequent omission of the subject, no distinction between singular and plural forms etc., I call the Japanese language's **repressive mode**, which contrast with the Western European languages' **expressive mode.** For example the Japanese sentence: 'Isha wa[d] gakusei wo[e] sukuu.' = '(The) doctor rescues (a) student.' Not considering the plural forms, this sentence can be translated into the following sixteen sentences in Dutch:

1. De dokter[f] redt een student[g]. 2. De dokter redt een studente[h]. 3. De dokteres[i] redt een student. 4. De dokteres redt een studente. 5. Een dokter redt een student. 6. Een dokter redt een studente. 7. Een dokteres redt een student. 8. Een dokteres redt een studente. 9. Een dokter redt de student. 10. Een dokter redt de studente. 11. Een dokteres redt de student. 12 Een dokteres redt de studente. 13. De dokter redt de student. 14. De dokter redt de studente. 15. De dokteres redt de student. 16. De dokteres redt de studente.

---

[c] In an artificial way genders can be distinguished in the Japanese language but it's almost never done.

[d] 'Wa', this participle indicates the nominative or subjective case.

[e] 'Wo', this participle indicates the accusative or objective case.

[f] 'dokter' means a male doctor.

[g] 'student' means a male student.

[h] 'studente' means a female student.

[I] 'dokteres' means a female doctor.

In Dutch language the distinguishing between plural and singular, indicating gender and using definite or indefinite articles, are necessary conditions to express oneself. Lack of these forms in the Japanese language can be explained only by a lack of need for them. For example, a society that doesn't know money, doesn't need words like currency, interest rate, and bank. The Japanese society, which is basically formed by stressing and enforcing the group 'harmony' shows this group's nature in its language.

Along with this 'group's nature', the Japanese language—society—attaches great importance to a person's social position: three words for 'to give' ('ageru', 'yaru', 'kudasaru') are used in Japanese, according to people's higher, equal or lower position. Special verbs are used when speaking to one's superior: for example the polite forms of 'to be', 'to do', and 'to come or to go' are 'gozaru', 'nasaru' and 'irrasharu'. The Japanese also show respect to others by prefixing the sound or letter 'o' or 'go' to a noun. This use of language according to people's social position exemplifies, once more, a highly stratified Japanese society: language use determined according to one's social position exemplifies similarly the repressive language mode; man isn't positioned on an equal level to freely use a common language.

Viewpoint of style. In 'Villon's Wife', the story's plot is set up by the referential meaning of 'The husband being hurried'. For what reason would a drunken husband open the front-door hurriedly? This ambiguity has an appetizing effect on the readers. 'Drunken' and 'in a hurry', 'the noise' and 'silently', 'woke up' and 'silently sleeping'; these pairs of contrasting words from the opening sentence create a contrastive atmosphere: establishes the appropriate mood for the story.

In summary, we have considered various referential meanings from various viewpoints. We learned what 'marriage', 'husband and wife' mean in Japanese society, knowledge we could use to better understand 'Villon's wife'. From a different language viewpoint, we found the Japanese repressive mode which is linked up with the highly stratified Japanese society. As for style we can notice that the writer starts with an exotic title followed by an opening sentence giving a full contrastive atmosphere: both can be considered as appetizers.

NOTES

1. The quoted passages from *Vyon no Tsuma*, (*Villon's Wife*), are from: Osamu Dazai, *Shayo-Ningen Shikkaku*, Tokyo, Shinchosha, 1997, pp. 246-266. Translated by W. Nuyten.

2. H. Tanaka, *The Japanese Legal System*, Tokyo, University of Tokyo Press, 1976, seventh printing 1988, p. 158

3. Ibid., p. 158.

4. Ibid., p. 158.

5. Demosthenes, Private Orations, In Nearam, Cambridge, Massachusetts, Harvard University.

6. F. Engels, *The Origin of the Family, Private Property and the State*, Karl Marx/ Frederick Engels, Collected Works Volume 26, New York, International Publishers, Copyright Progress Plublishers, Moscow, 1990, p. 188.

7. Hisako Kamata, *Onna no Chikara—Josei Minzoku Gakunyumon*, Tokyo, Seiga Shobo, 1990, pp. 52-55. Translated by W. Nuyten.

4

Meanings, Production and Discourse

Before we examine the next quotation from *Villon's Wife,* I will summarize the plot from the story's first part.

Missis' husband steals a lot of money from the café where he is a regular customer. He steals the money in a very simple way. While drinking in the café, the husband suddenly stands up and goes straight into the small inner-room of the café. Without saying a word, he forces the proprietress out of the way and opens a drawer. He grabs a wad of banknotes worth five thousand yen and thrusts it inside his double belt pocket. Then he quickly leaves the café. The prorietor couple follow the husband to his home, where they demand that he returns the stolen money. Ready to fight, the husband holds out his jackknife at the couple but he eventually flees the scene. Missis invites the proprietor couple inside and the three of them have a long conversation by which we learn that the husband is the second son of a baron and that he had become a famous poet after graduating from Tokyo Imperial University. The husband has a bad habit of spending a lot of money on liquor and women. In the next passage the proprietress is speaking about the second time when the husband visited her café during the Second World War.

> *'That evening he seemed to have been drinking a lot somewhere else before he came to our place. Standing he drank ten glasses of spirits. Although we tried to talk to him, he remained silent, smiling shyly and vaguely nodding in ascent. Suddenly he asked for the time and stood up.* [when he enterd the café, the husband had paid one hundred yen]
> "*The change,*" *I said but he answered,* "*No, that's okay.*" "*That puts me in an awkward position,*" *I said strongly. With a grin he told me to keep it for the next time and he left. However missis, that was the only time, for the first and last time, he paid us. Since then, we were deceived on one pretext or another for three years. Without paying a cent, he finished drinking all our liquor by himself That's why it's very disgusting. I couldn't help bursting into laughter. Without good reason I suddenly felt*

23

amused. Quickly I covered my mouth, but when I looked at the proprietress, she smiled in amusement and cast her eyes down. Then, the proprietor, too, couldn't help smiling bitterly. "Well it's not really a matter to laugh about; the unbelievable stupidity makes me want to laugh…"[1] [the proprietress continues talking]

From this passage we can deduce the following four referential meanings: 1. The husband has a habit of drinking a lot. 2. The husband is a bad-paying customer. 3. The proprietress' story is too pathetic. 4. Missis' response is lighthearted.

These referential meanings create the complete story's frame: the husband drinks like a fish; the proprietress talks exaggeratedly; and missis maintains a lighthearted mood. The same passage provides the next three hypothetical meanings: 1. The husband paid his bill only that one time. 2. After that one time, he drank the café's liquor over the next three years. 3. Missis was suddenly amused without good reason.

How do the referential meanings differ from the hypothetical meanings? Referential meanings are deduced from the text and are related to already known information that is provided by the context of the story. The hypothetical meanings are isolated, directly quoted meanings that are not necessarily true or real within the context of the story. It's worthwhile to notice that the first and second hypothetical meanings contradict the story's and also the world's reason. Can we find a man in this world who pays his café bill only once and then continues drinking all the café's liquor over the next three years? The third hypothetical meaning leaves room to draw inferences; it's constructive in developing the plot.

To get a deeper insight of the problems related to the various meanings I will leave the quoted passage as it is, and take a passage from Dostoyevsky's *Crime and Punishment*. The scene describes the last conversation between Raskolnikov (an ex-student) and Alyona Ivanova (a pawnbroker): it takes place just before Raskolnikov crushes her head with an axe. Raskolnikov was holding out his pledge to Alyona and she speaks to him:

> *'But why are you so pale? Look, your hands are shaking! Have you come out of a bath, dearie?'*
> *'It's fever,' he replied abruptly. 'One can't help looking pale…if one doesn't get anything to eat,' he added, barely able to get the words out. His strength was failing him again. But the reply had sounded convincing; the old woman took the pledge from him.*[2]

Referential meanings: 1. The old woman shows interest in Raskolnikov's sick appearance. 2. Raskolnikov's mental and physical health were weakened. 3. The old woman continues her work as a matter of routine.

Hypothetical meanings: 1. Raskolnikov has fever because he hasn't gotten anything to eat. 2. Raskolnikov's reply sounds convincing (so perhaps he doesn't speak the truth but lies).

Regular meanings: 1. When a student doesn't eat, he runs the risk of getting a fever. 2. It will be difficult for anyone who suffers from fever and/ or who doesn't eat to speak fluently.

The referential and regular meanings don't pose problems regarding the logic inside or outside the story. The hypothetical meanings partly agree with and partly contradict the regular and referential meanings. The reader knows that Raskolnikov's fever isn't caused by not having enough food but because he is about to kill the old woman.

The second hypothetical meaning supports the story's logic but in this case the meaning is created in a part of the text without quotation marks. This part of the text isn't in dialogue form, which can be produced only when the writer imagines himself or herself in his or her characters' position. Comments that the writer makes as the omniscient narrator emanate directly from the writer's thoughts and feelings.

Production processes. In the role of omniscient narrator, the writer passes through the process of consumption (from now on abbreviated C.) in which personal feelings and thoughts are converted—production (P.)—into the omniscient comments: the C. P.—process. Dialogues spring from a different production process: the writer creates (P.) various characters and imagines (C.) his characters' feelings and thoughts after which he produces (P'.) their dialogues: this is the P.C.P.—process.

The next quotation is from Osamu Dazai's story *Ogon Fukei* (*Golden Scenery*). For this autobiographical story O. Dazai used his life-experience of three years before he wrote the story. That time, he was recuperating from lung problems and appendicitis, addicted to morphine and deep in debt.

> *'The year before last, I was expelled from my family and reduced to poverty overnight. I was left wandering the streets, begging help from various quarters, barely being able to stay alive from one day to the next, and just when I began to think that I might support myself by writing, I fell seriously ill.* [3]

Referential meanings: 1. Dazai's health and financial situation were very bad. 2. Dazai was on bad terms with his family.

Hypothetical meanings: 1. After being expelled from his family, Dazai could barely stay alive. 2. He began to think that he might support himself by writing.

The above mentioned referential and hypothetical meanings agree with the story's logic and O. Dazai's life. Although Dazai's family rented a house for him in Tokyo and sent him a monthly allowance; he was on worse terms with his family than ever before. It must have been extremely difficult for a morphine-addicted Dazai to provide himself a living during the period described in the story. For an outsider, being expelled may sound exaggerated when the family still rents a house for him and sends an allowance, but departing from Dazai's personal life (addicted, sick, lusting after a literary prize) this feeling of 'being expelled' is realistic.

The thought that he might support himself by writing wasn't a castle in the air. Dazai was nominated for the first Akutagawa Prize (the most prestigious prize for Japanese writers) in the summer of 1935. Unfortunately, because of his image as a drug-addict, he didn't receive the prize. For the same reason, he failed to win the second Akutagawa Prize in 1936.

Autobiographical material is a product of the C.P.—process, but when we deal with **fictional** autobiographical material it's the product of the P.C.P.—process: for example a writer must create and absorb a fictional narrator. When we reconsider the second quotation from *Villon's Wife* in which the café proprietress talks exaggeratedly and missis bursts out laughing at the end, we observe that Dazai has firmly rooted himself in missis as the omniscient narrator. This identification of the writer with the heroine who takes the place of the omniscient narrator is immediately visible because her narration isn't enclosed in quotation marks.

Discourse. (for cross-reference about discourses; *Marxism and The Philosophy of Language* by V.N. Volosinov). We have to consider discourse 'originator' and, according to different originators distinguish various kinds of discourses. I will add my definition of discourse: a continuous stretch of language (oral or written), that doesn't necessarily overlap a sentence or a paragraph, but contains enough information to treat it as an independent unit of subject-matter. Now I will lay bare a number of distinct discourses from the 'other's language perspective'. For this purpose I will quote from Osamu Dazai's work (English translation and the Japanese text), from Dostoyevsky (English translation and Japanese translation), and finally from Charles Dickens (English text).

A1
"I wondered if the feeling I experienced then was what people mean by the well-worn phrase "dignity of human life. [4]

A2

If I were to express my feelings in words, it would have been something like "It can't be helped." [5]

A3

I cannot possibly think of it in terms of a "hideous mistake" or anything of the sort. [6]

B1

"That Dazai fellow's awfully frivolous these days, "they sneer."
"He tries to garner readers simply by amusing; he doesn't put any effort into his writing at all." [7]

B2

the husband and wife treat each other with kindness and respect and have never engaged in a single reckless argument of the "Get out!" "I'm leaving!" variety, much less physical violence, [8]

C

'I plan to attempt a thing like this, yet I allow that kind of rubbish to scare me!' he thought with a strange smile. 'Hm…yes…Everything lies in a man's hands, [9]

Now I will give the original Japanese text of A1, A2, A3, B1, B2 and the Japanese translation (from the Russian text) of C.

a1
人生の厳粛とは、こんなときの感じを言うのであろうか、[10]
a2
仕方がない。
言葉で言いあらわすなら、そんな感じのものだった。[11]
a3
けがらわしい失策などとは、どうしても私には思われません。[12]
b1
太宰という作家も、このごろは軽薄である、おもしろさだけで読者を釣る、
すこぶる安易、と私をさげすむ。[13]
b2
夫婦はいたわり、尊敬しあい、夫は妻を打ったことなど無いのはむろん、[14]
出てゆけ、出てゆきますなどの、乱暴な口争いをしたことさえ一度もなかったし、
c
『あれだけのことを断行しようと思っているのに、 こんなくだらないことで
びくつくなんて！』 奇妙な微少を浮かべながら、 彼はこう考えた。
『ふうん！‥‥そうだ‥‥いっさいの事は人間の筆中にあるんだが、[15]

Passages a1, a2, and a3 show that words and phrases are separated in a natural way—by comma—in a Japanese text. The double quotation marks in the English translations A1, A2 and A3 are unnecessary inventions of the English translator. The fourth quotation, b1, is written by Dazai in the indirect-speech form. From a sea of gossip about him, Dazai chooses some examples. To insert 'they' in the English translation B1, is superfluous and the quotation marks are fundamentally wrong. The correct translation is as follows: 'These days I'm looked down upon as a frivolous writer, who tries only to lure readers by amusing; far too easy.'

The translator from B1 uses a style that is too 'free' and not 'true' to the original. A possible explanation for the incorrect English translation might be the working of the expressive mode in English. Since the repressive mode in Japanese language creates vagueness—the slipping away of meanings—likewise the expressive mode in English tends to create exaggerations and untruths.

Similarly, the translation B2 is too free. 'Physical violence' ought to be—according to the Japanese text—translated as 'at no time did the husband strike his wife, of course,'...

The English translation C1 treats Raskolnikov's inner-speech exactly the same as direct speech by using single quotation marks. In the Japanese translation, c1, Raskolnikov's inner-speech is correctly distinguished from direct speech by using double quotation marks.

Quasi author's discourse. In the previous example Raskolnikov's inner-speech was made visible by quotation marks. This isn't always the case. A character's inner-speech can be a part of the author's discourse. The following sentence from *Crime and Punishment* is an example:

> *This was the one respect in which he admitted to any crime: in not having had the courage of his convictions and in having turned himself in.* [16]

It looks like author's discourse but, the message comes straight from the character. The sentence can easily be changed in character's discourse: This was the one respect in which I admitted to any crime: I didn't have the courage of my convictions and turned myself in. This type of discourse I call quasi author's discourse; the form and presentation makes it look like author's discourse, but the message belongs to a character. The next sentence is an example of absolute authorial discourse, because the message can belong only to the author. The sentence is from the same passage as the sentence quoted above.

> *He didn't understand that his sense might have been the harbinger of the future crises in his life, of his future recovery, his new vision of life.* [17]

Quasi character's discourse. Most of Osamu Dazai's 'fictional' autobiographical writings are in quasi character's discourse; the message, being delivered by a character, is a direct experience, feeling, thought etc. from Dazai's life. The author's message is hidden in his character's discourse. I will give two quotations from Dazai's novel *The Setting Sun* in which the character's discourse is firmly based on Dazai's personal experience and thoughts. The quotations are passages from the heroine's brother Naoji's testament:

> *It's no use. I'm going first. I completely don't understand why I ought to go on living.*
> *Only people who wish to go on living should do so. Just as a man has the right to live, he also must have the right to die.* [18]
> *I wanted to become coarse. Strong, no I wanted to be brutal. I thought that was the only way I would be able to become the so-called people's friend. Liquor wasn't of any use. I always had to feel a spinning dizziness. For this I had no other choice but to take drugs. I had to forget my family. I had to oppose my father's blood.* [19]

Pseudo objective discourse. The following quotation is from Charles Dickens' novel *Oliver Twist*:

> *Oliver bowed low by the direction of the beadle, and was then hurried away to a large ward, where, on a rough, hard bed, he sobbed himself to sleep.*
> *What a noble illustration of the tender laws of this favoured country!*
> *They let the paupers go to sleep.* [20]

The sentence 'What a noble country...' is presented as author's discourse, but it doesn't present C. Dickens' view about The Poor Laws in England', which he personally, abhorred. The origin of this sentence is situated in the hypocritical bourgeoisie's ideology: the laws were made by them and for their own benefit. C. Dickens speaks in the form of parody:

'They let the paupers go to sleep!' This parody unmasks the hypocrisy of the previous sentence 'What a noble illustration of the tender laws of this favoured country!'

NOTES

1. The quoted passages from *Vyon no Tsuma*, (*Villon's Wife*) are from: Osamu Dazai, *Shayo-Ningen Shikkaku*, Tokyo, Shinchosha, 1979, pp. 246-266. Translated by W. Nuyten.

2. F. Dostoyevsky, *Crime and Punishment*, England, Penguin Classics, 1991, p. 113.

3. Osamu Dazai, *Ogon Fukei, Kirigirisu*, Tokyo, Shinchosha, 1974, p. 45. Translated by W. Nuyten.

4. Osamu Dazai, *The Setting Sun*, translated by Donald Keene, Tokyo, Charles E. Tuttle Co., 1992, Copyright 1956 by New Directions Publishing Company, p. 20.

5. Ibid., p. 148.

6. Ibid., p. 172.

7. Osamu Dazai, *Self Portraits,* translated by Ralf F. McCarthy, Tokyo, Kodansha International, 1992, p. 224.

8. Ibid., p. 225.

9. F. Dostoyevsky, *Crime and Punishment*, England, Penguin Classics, 1991, p. 33.

10. Osamu Dazai, *Shayo-Ningen Shikkaku*, Tokyo, Shinchosha, 1979, p. 17.

11. Ibid., p. 89.

12. Ibid., p. 100.

13. Osamu Dazai *Otto (Cherries)*, Osamu Dazai Collected Works, Tokyo, Shueisha, 1972, p. 379.

14. Ibid., p. 379.

15. F. Dostoyevsky, *Crime and Punishment*, (*Tsumi to Batsu*), translator M. Ogawa, Tokyo, Kawade Shobo Shinsha, copyright 1969, p. 5.

16. F. Dostoyevsky, *Crime and Punishment*, England, P enguin Classics, 1991, p. 623.

17. Ibid., 624.

18. Osamu Dazai, *Shayo*, (*The Setting Sun*), Osamu Dazai Collected Works, Shueisha, Tokyo, 1972, p. 99. Translated by W. Nuyten.

19. Ibid., p. 100.

20. Charles Dickens, *Oliver Twist*, England, Penguin Books, edition 1983, p. 83.

5

Moral Classification

Let's take up the thread of the story *Villon's Wife*. The day after the husband's quarrel with the café proprietors, missis goes with her two or three-year-old son to the café. She lies to the proprietors that she will be able to return the money which had been stolen by her husband. Missis promises to work in the café for as long as the stolen money isn't returned. That same evening, her husband in the company of a thirty-four-year old woman, suddenly turns up in the café. The husband and this woman return the stolen money to the proprietor while missis is at work. After her husband and the woman leave, missis decides to continue working in the café. During these first weeks of work at the café, missis enjoys her new, active life, but she also notices the mercenary side of society's morals. After working one month, missis accomodates a first-time customer of the café at her home. Her husband being absent as usual, missis makes love with this customer at daybreak. That morning she goes with her son to the café, where her husband sits at a table, with a glass of liquor, reading the newspaper. He explains missis that because of last night's heavy rainfall he had stayed overnight at the café. Then this last scene follows:

> *'Perhaps I will also take up my lodgings in this café permanently.' [missis] 'That's all right; however.' [husband] 'Let's do so. Renting our house forever is meaning-less.' My husband silently gazed at the newspaper again. 'Ah, again they've written maliciously about me: an epicurean, fake aristocrat. That fellow misses the mark. He should better talk about a God-fearing epicurean. Sachan, look here. I'm described as a brute of a man. It's not so, is it? Although I tell it now, the five thou-sand yen I took from the café last year, I had intended to spend on a Happy New Year with Sachan and my boy. Since I'm not a brute of a man, I could do such a thing.' I didn't feel particularly happy, 'A brute of a man is also fine, as long as we manage to survive,' I answered.* [1]

This passage gives the following meanings; Referential meanings: 1. Missis and her husband reach agreement to move into the café. 2. The husband, because

32

of his life-style (from the context) is described as an epicurean, fake aristocrat. 3. Missis isn't really interested in hearing her husband's explanation about his character, behavior and intentions.

Hypothetical meanings: 1. The husband had 'taken' five thousand yen from the café, to spend on a Happy New Year with his wife and boy. 2. He took the money since he isn't a brute of a man.

This last sentence of 'Villon's Wife' I will compare with a passage from the epilogue of *Crime and Punishment*.

> *'After all, why does what I [Raskolnikov] did seem so outrageous to them?' he said to himself. 'Because it was an act of wickedness? But what do they mean, those words: "an act of wickedness"? My conscience is easy. Of course from a legal point of view a crime was committed; of course, the letter of the law was violated and blood was spilt, well then, here is my head, take it in exchange for the letter of the law...and let that be that! Though of course in that case a great many of mankind's benefactors who did not inherit power but took it for themselves ought to have been executed at their very first steps. But those people had the courage of their convictions, and so they were right, while I didn't, and, consequently had no right to take the steps I did.' This was the one respect in which he admitted to any crime: in not having had the courage of his convictions and in having turned himself in.* [2]

I deduce the following meanings from this passage; Referential meanings: 1. Raskolnikov confuses the relation of crime and law; a certain type of crime produces a corresponding law. He didn't violate 'the letter of the law' but he violated the human right of others to be alive. 2. Raskolnikov doesn't show much remorse for his murder. 3. According to Raskolnikov, every strong man is his own master with disregard for society's laws.

Hypothetical meanings: 1. Raskolnikov admits to the crime of not having had the courage of his convictions and in having turned himself in. 2. Is the killing of that—"loathsome, harmful louse; a filthy old money lender woman"—page 595– old woman an act of wickedness?

I will classify the foregoing referential and hypothetical meanings from *Villon's Wife* and *Crime and Punishment* according to the various forms of discourse, speech form and production process.

Villon's Wife

Referential meanings:

1. Missis and her husband reach agreement to move into the café.

↗ direct speech
→ quasi-character's discourse
↘ P. C. 'P' [a]

2. The husband is because of his life-style described as an epicurean, fake aristocrat.

↗ direct speech
→ quasi-character's discourse
↘ P. C. 'P'

3. Missis isn't really interested in hearing her husband's explanation about etc.

↗ indirect speech
→ quasi-character's discourse
↘ P. C. 'P'

Hypothetical meanings:

1. The husband had taken five thousand yen from the café, to spend on a Happy New Year with his wife and boy.

↗ direct speech
→ quasi-character's discourse
↘ P. C. 'P'

2. He took the money since he isn't a brute of a man.

↗ direct speech
→ quasi-character's discourse
↘ P. C. 'P'

Crime and Punishment

Referential meanings:

1. Raskolnikov confuses the relation between crime and law; a certain type of crime etc.

↗ direct speech
→ character's discourse
↘ P. C. P.

2. Raskolnikov doesn't show much remorse for his murder.

↗ direct speech
→ character's discourse
↘ P. C. P.

3. According to Raskolnikov is every strong man his own master with disregard for society's laws.

↗ direct speech
→ character's discourse
↘ P. C. P.

Hypothetical meanings:

1. Raskolnikov admits to the crime of not having had the courage of his convictions and in having turned himself in.

↗ direct speech
➔ quasi-author's discourse
↘ P. C. P.

2. Is the killing of that old woman an act of wickedness?

↗ indirect speech
➔ character's discourse
↘ P. C. P.

---

[a] We have observed a number of times that Osamu Dazai's work is mainly fictional-auto-biographical. Dazai first creates (produces) a narrator with whom he consumes his thoughts, feelings etc., then he produces his writings. The production of the narrator may cause the loss of the perspective from the other when the writer and his or her hero or heroine dissolve themselves in the omniscient narrator. Hereby it's no longer possible to distinguish which material is pure fictional and which material is autobiographical: for this reason I marked the second part of the production process by single quotation marks, 'P'.

Besides the previous classification, I will give a moral classification of the previously used referential and hypothetical meanings. The four values of true–untrue, good–evil, I use from two perspectives: 1. the discourse carrier, and 2. the public moral.

The discourse carrier perspective: in the case of quasi-character's discourse—*Villon's Wife*—I consider the writer himself to be the discourse carrier, likewise in the case of quasi author's discourse I regard the character as the the discourse carier.

The public moral perspective: this is a very vague means, however, election results, purchasing trends, mass media moral etc. might provide us with indications and clues to the public's moral.

To illustrate how I classify the moral values of the various meanings, I will reason aloud about the first hypothetical meaning that I deduced from *Crime and Punishment*: if Raskolnikov would have had the courage of his convictions; he should have had the right to kill the old woman. Raskolnikov reaches the conclusion that he didn't have the courage of his convictions. This means a personal defeat for him. His purpose in life to be a Napoleon and his mental frame work are destroyed. Accordingly, the message from the first hypothetical meaning is true for Raskolnikov. And the outcome of this realisation—turning himself in—leads to his deportation to Siberia, which is evil for Raskolnikov.

Without checking data that could provide insight into the Russian public moral of 1860, I don't think it is permissible in any civilized society to murder someone for the sake of proving to be a Napoleon (= the courage of his convictions). That's why the public would never consider 'not having had the courage of his convictions' as a crime, which makes this hypothetical meaning untrue. The outcome from this hypothetical meaning that results in Raskolnikov's imprisonment can be considered as good according to public moral, because a person who commits such a brutal, senseless murder deserves severe punishment.

story title	meanings	no	discourse carrier moral	Public moral
Villon's Wife	Referential meanings	(1)	true good	true bad
		(2)	true bad	true good
		(3)	true bad	true good
	Hypothetical meanings	(1)	true good	(un)true bad
		(2)	true good	untrue bad
Crime and Punishment	Referential meanings	(1)	untrue bad	true bad
		(2)	true good	true bad
		(3)	true good	untrue bad
	Hypothetical meanings	(1)	true bad	untrue good
		(2)	untrue good	true bad

The moral classification schedule clearly shows that the discourse carrier's moral clashes with the public moral on all referential and hypothetical meanings.

Instead of comparing two passages, it might be more fruitful to compare an infinite number of passages. However a human life isn't infinite, which makes it impossible to carry out this plan. Yet, I will take one more passage from Ogai Mori (1862–1922). The story is entitled *Seinen* (1910), which translates as *Young Man*. The story's main character and narrator is Junichi.

30 November. Fair weather. It's strange to write every day about the weather as writing in my diary. I can't keep writing my diary every day. The other day, when I visited Oomura, we talked about this and he said, 'Since you have to follow so many rules every day, you don't have to restrict yourself on top of this.' Just because you're living, you don't need to go to the trouble of keeping a diary every day. The problem is what to do without having to write my diary. It's a problem as to what purpose I can free myself. To be alive. To live. The answer is simple, but the contents, incidently, aren't simple.

......

Do Japanese people know the meaning of 'living'? As soon as people enter the gate of elementary school, they try so hard just to go through school. Getting a job, you try to do a thorough job; you think that is life. But there is no life. The present is a dividing line between past and future. If there's no life on this line, there's no life anywhere. Then, what am I doing?[3]

Referential meanings: 1. Junichi feels it a duty to continue writing his diary every day. 2. Junichi loses his purpose in life after having listened to his friend's advice. 3. Junichi can't understand the meaning of his life.

Hypothetical meanings: 1. Since you have to follow so many rules every day, you don't have to restrict yourself on top of this. 2. Do Japanese people know the meaning of 'living'? 3. The present is a dividing line between past and future; so if there's no life on this line, there's no life anywhere.

Once more, I will reason aloud to show how I ascertain the moral value of, for example, the second hypothetical meaning. Junichi, the discourse carrier, has strong doubts about there being life. Consequently, he asks himself, 'Then, what am I doing?' Junichi, being Japanese, doesn't know the meaning of 'living' so it must be untrue for him that Japanese people know the meaning of 'living'. This hypothetical meaning produces a negative effect; Junichi loses his purpose in life.

Making a judgement about the public moral of 'living' is a difficult problem. Most people are continuously searching for the meaning of 'living', and as far as I know, no one was able to give a perfect answer. Though Junichi gave the answer that Japanese people, including himself, don't know the meaning of 'living'. I don't think this problem can be grasped by the human mind: we should leave this problem to our creator. For this reason, I will leave the general public moral for the second hypothetical meaning blank.

story title	meanings	no	discourse carrier moral		Public moral	
Seinen	Referential meanings	(1)	true	bad	true	bad
		(2)	true	bad	true	bad
		(3)	true	bad	true	bad
	Hypothetical meanings	(1)	true	bad	true	good
		(2)	untrue	bad	×	×
		(3)	true	bad	untrue	bad

We have analysed three passages from which we can conclude that:

1. Quasi character discourse is linked up with the production process of P.C. 'P'.

2. It is impossible to make a clear distinction between fictional and autobiographical writings when the writer and his hero or heroine dissolve themselves in the omniscient narrator.

3. The two forms of speech—direct and indirect—don't influence in any particular way the various referential and hypothetical meanings and their moral classification.

4. In Dazai's and Dostoyevsky's literature, we found many contrasts between the discourse carrier and the public moral for the various meanings.

5. The reason I don't consider *Seinen* a literary work is the almost complete lack of these contrasts between the discourse carrier and public moral.
   Drawing on these conclusions I can formulate a ninth mechanism that is at work in literature and literary production.

9. While a writer uses various techniques—choice of discourse and speech type—bases his or her writing on different production processes: it's the contrast between the discourse carrier and the public moral values for the various meanings that has to be the essenttial ingredient of his or her literature.

NOTES

1. Osamu Dazai, *Villon's' Wife, Shayo-Ningen Shikkaku*, Tokyo, Shincho-sha, 1979, p. 266, translated by W. Nuyten.

2. Dostoyevsky, *Crime and Punishment*, England, Penguin Books, 1991, p. 623.

3. Oogai Mori, *Seinen (Young Man)*, Oogai Mori Collected Works, Tokyo, Shueisha, 1973, pp. 191-192, translated by L.G. Perkins.

6

The Element of Movement and the Relation between Society and Language

In the first part of this chapter I will describe the element of movement in literary works. Hereto I will plug into new material: 1. *Ochiba no Tonari* ('The neighbor of fallen leaves') is a story written by S. Yamamoto in 1959. The story's main characters are three children,—Shigeji, Sankichi and Ohisa—who grow up in the same workmen's neighborhood in Tokyo. The story's theme is the development of relationships, based on friendship, love and trust among these characters. 2. *Circus* is a short story written by Yukio Mishima in 1949. The story is about a circuss boss and one of his employees who plan and carry out the 'accidental' death of a young-lover couple that belongs to the circus staff.

Let's start with the opening passage from *Ochiba no Tonari*:

> *Ohisa always had Shigeji on her mind. That was very obvious from the beginning. However, Shigeji, who from the bottom of his heart, burned with love for Ohisa, was too timid. While not hearing Ohisa's explicit word, Shigeji believed that Ohisa was in love with Sankichi, which completely wore him out.* [1]

Regular meaning: regardless of our own will, destiny plays its own independent role in our lives.

Referential meaning: Shigeji hurts his own feelings of affection for Ohisa because of his disposition.

Hypothetical meaning: Ohisa was in love with Sankichi.

The regular meaning provides us with the—traditionally called—theme of the story. This theme, which we were able to deduce from the opening passage, won't show any development, for which reason I leave it as it is.

The referential meaning, which we deduced from the opening passage, connects in story-time with the end of the story when the main characters are grown-ups. After the openings passage, the writer goes back to the three friends' childhood. With little jumps in time—intervals of a couple of years—the writer gives flesh and blood to the referential meaning. The relation among the three friends exists at first only in space: they are born in the same apartment house. Although Shigeji and Sankichi are the same age, they hardly know each other till a certain incident occurs that links them with Ohisa. Shigeji and Sankichi are twelve, and Ohisa is seven at the time of the incident. The incident occurs along the river, which flows near the neighborhood where the main characters live. While catching crabs along the river, Ohisa is being teased by a group of boys. They knock over her bucket with crabs. Shigeji, who hears Ohisa crying, comes to her rescue but he is too weak to confront the group of boys. At that moment Sankichi appears and tells the boys to stop bullying Ohisa and Shigeji. The boys obey Sankichi's authoritative command and leave the scene. The three main characters are then placed in a mutual relationship. The story and the life of the three characters really take off from this incident.

The writer provides only meagre information about their earlier childhood. The bullying incident, which forms the point of departure for their relationship, also clearly marks the friends' characters: Sankichi being strong, adult and independent; Shigeji being helpful, impulsive and lacking confidence; Ohisa being the girl in need of help and love. From the moment of the incident, the story is propelled forward by the force of time. The writer continuously uses 'time' to introduce a new event:

> *When Shigeji was twelve years old, his father died. From then, three years later…At the age of nineteen, in November…At the age of twenty-four, in March…When it became summer.*

The story moves along by time: the writer must have consciously chosen to let events evolve around the axis of time. The pre-arranged space in the story —apartment house, neighborhood, river—remains unchanged and functions like the blackcloth in a theatre. If the writer had situated Ohisa in a different quarter of the city (and in a different social position), the basis of shared equality by the three friends would have been missing. It would have become a different story. In *Ochiba no Tonari* the presence of shared equality in the same environment guarantees a concentration on the purity of love and friendship among the characters. When we recall *The Izu Dancer*, the moving forces in that story are **space** and time. The encounter of the student with the troupe of strolling entertainers on the **road** is an especially important feature. The road is open to everyone, people of different social positions and ages are moving along the road. The story develops along the road and it's the student's departure by ship, in the end, that sharply breaks off, in space, his relation with the troupe of strolling entertainers.

The hypothetical meaning 'Ohisa was in love with Sankichi', is partly worked out in unchanged space and further developed by the axis of time. Though space, like a blackcloth, never functions as the moving force of this hypothetical meaning. Concludingly, the moving force in *Ochiba no Tonari* is the presentation of events according to the writer's pre-arranged time axis.

Turning our attention to Yukio Mishima's short story *Circus*, we find a different type of moving force; silence-noise:

1.   *The circus boss remained silent while, by one hand drawing triangles and squares in the air with his whip. At a time like this, he was angry.*

2.   *Without saying anything, the circuss boss twisted the couple's arms.*

3.   *The circus boss nodded.*

4.   *The band's trumpets suddenly blew high pitched.*

5.   *The audience sobbed and cheered frantically.*

6.   *The circus boss didn't answer.*

7.   *The band abruptly stopped playing.*

8.   *That time the sound of hoofs could be heard outside the tent.* [2]

The frequent silent moments of the circus boss, the intervals of silence and noise that are created by the audience and the band, and finally the sound of hoofs—indicating the coming of the couple's funeral procession—are subtly used movement enforcement elements. I think that it is up to the writer's ingenuity to employ different and new axes of movement enforcements.

Relation between society and language. So far, we observed that the writer, his or her life and his or her literary works, are interwoven with the surrounding society. By analysing literary works (whether connected with or disconnected from the writer) we are able to expose ideological, political, economical etc. mechanisms that are at work in society.

In studying *The Izu Dancer* we noticed that Y. Kawabata fixed his characters' social position by the contents of language and the degree of politeness expressed by the characters speeches related to each other. The relation between language use and the speaker's or listener's position can be more complicated in ordinary life than in a literary work. Independent from social position, the same language can be used by different classes. A separate layer within a class may use the same ideological language: the language of lawyers, the language of artists, the language of priests etc. Diverse ideological languages might be used by one and the same person. And languages might signify different meanings depending on the situation and by whom they are used. Karl Marx assumed a causal chain-connection between language and social position: 'Ideas do not exist apart from language'[3] and 'The ideas of the ruling class are in every epoch the ruling ideas, i.e., the class which is the ruling material force of society is at the same time its ruling intellectual force.' [4] We can summarize the meanings of these quotations in a Marxist thesis about language: 1. Class struggle influences language.[a]

How did class struggle influence the changing meanings of the word 'family'? The original meaning of family is the total number of slaves belonging to one man. The Romans defined family as the total number of slaves—servants— belonging to the head of a household, and all the persons related to him by blood or marriage. When making a jump in time, F. Engels argued in 1884 that the bourgeois marriage, based on a material foundation—economic interests—could be distinguished from the really freely contracted marriages, based on mutual sex love and free agreement, among the oppressed class. Engels states that the inequality of the partners, originating in earlier social conditions, continues especially in the bourgeois marriage. 'In the family, he [the husband] is the bourgeois, the wife represents the proletariat.' [5] The slave-element in the Roman definition disappears from Engels' definition and instead marriage is linked with class and economic interests.

In 1949, the anthropologist G. Murdock gave the following definition of family: 'a social group characterized by common residence, economic cooperation and reproduction. It includes adults of both sexes, at least two of whom maintain a socially approved sexual relationship and one or more children, own or adopted, of the sexually cohabiting adults.' [6]

Murdock's definition replaces 'class interest' with 'economic cooperation'. The inequality of the partners in a bourgeois marriage and the free 'mutual sex love' marriage among the oppressed gives way to a 'socially approved sexual relationship'. The inner-functions of the family such as the dependence of the wife on her husband, and children's development possibilities that are linked with their family's social position, are all mystified in Murdock's definition.

In summary, the development from slave-based marriage, class-economic based bourgeois marriage and the mutual sex love marriage among the oppressed and finally the residential-economic reproductional group, reflects changes in the meaning and functioning of the family caused by the outcome of class struggle: feudalism; master and slave, capitalism; bourgeois and proletarian, imperialism; monopoly capitalist and world proletarian. The most current meaning of words—language—conform to the ideas of the ruling class of that epoch and might be determined by that ruling class.

---

[a] I consider literary production as an integral part of modern languages.

Premises of history. Marx and Engels formulated the following premises of history in *The German Ideology.* [7]

1. *The first historical act is thus the production of the means to satisfy these needs [eating, drinking, etc.], the production of material life itself.*

2. *The satisfaction of the first need, the action of satisfying and the instrument of satisfaction which has been required, leads to new needs,*

3. *Men begin to make other men, to procreate their kind,…*

4. *The production of life [natural-social], . . [which] is always combined with a certain mode of co-operation, or social stage and this mode of co-operation is itself a "productive force".*

5. *The determination of consciousness by men's physical organisation and by men's certain way of producing their life causes that 'The mind is from the outset afflicted with the curse of being "burdened" with matter,'*

Hereby, I propose my set of premises of history:

1. The first historical act is the 'birth' of speech in primitive men.

2. The development of speech into language must have been accompanied by a growth in men's consciousness.

3. The increased speech ability and consciousness by which man starts to distinguish himself from other animals, brings forth the organisation of men's social life, wich takes place in a reciprocal relation with the formation and development of various modes of production.

4. Language—consciousness—is the one and only medium to form and express individual and class—consciousness; it is the primary medium for generating ideas and ideology.

5. The determination of productive modes in a reciprocal relation with and by men's consciousness—language—results in:
    Matter afflicted with the curse of being burdened with language!

Departing from my premises, it follows that language constitutes itself as the motive force of men's history, of men's society. It is only by language that we acquire consciousness which enables us to build up and participate in social and productive environments.

It's by language that K. Marx became aware of the ever growing acute class conflicts in capitalist society. By language K. Marx was able to acquire knowledge about the political and economical mechanisms that are at work in capitalist society. It was by language that K. Marx and his followers influenced the thoughts and actions of the working class. After having left this world, K. Marx and F. Engels continue to influence our thoughts and actions by their writings, which contain their ideas, their ideology, their **language.**

From my premises of history and accompanying observations, I can deduce the second thesis about language, which forms the antithesis of the first Marxist thesis: 2. Languages—ideological languages—influences the class struggle.

Disconnection between 'being' and 'consciousness'. Marx and Engels identify a unity of material-social activity and language:

> *The production of ideas, of conceptions, of consciousness is at first directly interwoven with the material activity and the material intercourse of men—the language of real life.* [8]

Marx and Engels write about mankind in its early stages of existence, while I will consider the present day. In the Japanese language of the twentieth century we notice the use of many Japanized-English words like strike, boss and salary. These words written in 'Katakana' (see the footnotes) the square Japanese syllabary used for writing foreign names and words, have their original equivalents in traditional Japanese: strike ('domei higyo'), boss ('oyakata') and salary ('kyuryo'). It's perhaps inconspicuous but Japanized-English words cause changes in the—connotative—meaning. For example the word 'demonstration' can be translated into the original Japanese 'ijii-undo', or in the Japanized-English 'demo'. The original Japanese word 'iji-undo' is appropriate when talking about the 1969 Paris revolution, in which students almost overthrew the French government. The Japanized-English word 'demo' can be used when students demonstrate against the closure of their school's cafeteria. Also some words lose their original meanings. The Japanese word 'aware' lost it previous meanings of 'cheerful emotion' and 'love, deep attachment' and kept only some of its gloomy meanings such as 'pity', 'sad' and 'miserable'.

Besides meanings disappearing, we have new meanings and words created: Marxism, software, e-mail, and Japanimation. Words can have several meanings; words can take on new meanings and lose old and present meanings. Words can disappear and new words can be made; but the act of attaching a **specific meaning** to an existing word—or a group of words—I call signifying meaning. Now we will confront a negative effect of incorrectly signifying meaning.

In Japanese language, middle class is described as the class having an income in the middle (usual Japanese Dictionary); and most Japanese people think they belong to the middle class. When using hard figures[9] we find a completely different reality: in 1979, 48.89% of laborers, 59.01% of salaried office employees, 42.03% of petty bourgeoisie, 43.24% of individual proprietors, 34.7% of corporate executives, 40.59% of professionals and 20.11% of those with no occupation, received a yearly income between \3.2 and \6.0 million (based on more-than-one person households). We can present the same figures the following way: 51.01% of laborers, 40.99% of salaried office employees, 57.97% of petty bourgeoisie, 56.76% of individual proprietors, 65.30% of corporation executives, etc. fall outside the very widely stretched yearly income bracket of \3.2 to \6.0 million. Close to an average of 60% of all households fall outside the foregoing yearly income bracket; however, the majority of the Japanese people position themselves in the middle class.

Most Japanese adults not being aware of incorrect use of expressions like 'middle class', 'my home' etc., reflects the existense of a non-critical consciousness among them. Capitalist society will be able to survive as long as this non-critical consciousness is untouched and preserved.

strike（ストライキ）＝ 'domei higyo' 同盟罷業
boss（ボス）＝ 'oyakata' 親方
salary（サラリー）＝ 'kyuryo' 給料
demonstration（デモ）＝ 'ijii-undo' 示威運動
aware　哀れ

It's the act of incorrectly signifying words—language—that creates a false consciousness by which people aren't able anymore to connect 'being' and 'consciousness'. Formation of consciousness based on misleading, vague and incorrect meanings, makes people think and act contradictory to their own interest and social postion; it's this phenomenon[a] which I call the disunity of material-social activity and language. This leads us to the formulation of the third thesis about language: 3. Incorrectly signifying meaning causes disunity between material-activity and language.

---

[a] This phenomenon was underestimated by K. Marx and F. Engels due to their reinterpretation of Hegel's dialectics. Hegel's world spirit, which effects the dialectical progression of world history, was replaced in Marxism by the dialectics of productive forces and productive relations that effect the eventually possible progression of world history.

In summary, the three Marxist theses about langauge can be added to the previously formulated mechanisms that are at work in literature and literary production because literary production is an integral part of modern languages.

10. Class struggle influences language (and literary production).

11. Language (ideological language) influences class struggle.

12. Incorrectly signifying meaning is the source of the disunity between material—social activity and language.

NOTES

1. Shuguro Yamamoto *Ochiba no Tonari*, Collected Works, Tokyo, Shinchosha, 1982, pp. 283-311. Translated by W. Nuyten.

2. Yukio Mishima, *Circus*, (*Manatsu no Shi*), Tokyo, Shinchosha, 1970, pp. 70-79. Translated by W. Nuyten.

3. Karl Marx/ Frederick Engels, Collected Works Volume 28, New York, International Publishers, Copyright Progress Publishers, Moscow, 1986, p. 99.

4. Karl Marx/ Frederick Engels, *The German Ideology*, Collected Works Volume 5, Moscow, Progress Publishers 1976, p. 59.

5. F. Engels, *The Origin of the Family, Private Property and the State*, Karl Marx/ Frederick Engels, Collected Works Volume 26, New York, International Publishers, Copyright Progress Publishers Moscow, 1990, p. 181.

6. The Blackwell Dictionary of Social Thought, Oxford, England Blackwell, Publishers, 1993, p. 220.

7. Karl Marx/ Frederick Engels, Collected Works Volume 5, *The German Ideology*, Moscow, Progress Publishers, 1976, pp. 42-44.

8. Ibid., p. 36.

9. R. Steven, *Classes in Contemporary Japan,* Table 1.4, England, Cambridge University. Press, 1983.

PART 2

LITERARY THEORY
AND
AN ANALYSIS

1

Some Critics

The Russian Formalists, writers, artists and critics groups, that formed the Moscow Linguistic Circle (1915) and the St. Petersburg group (1916), initiated modern literary theory. Roman Jakobson was the most famous Moscow Linguistic Circle's member, and Victor Shklovsky was the Opayas group leader in St.Petersburg. In 1920, Jakobson moved to Czechoslovakia, where he helped to found the Prague Linguistic Circle.

Both Jakobson and Shklovsky based their literary theories on the linguistics framework derived from the Swiss linguist Ferdinand de Saussure (1857–1913). Saussure, who is widely regarded as the father of modern linguistics, expounded his theory during three courses of lectures on general linguistics at the University of Geneva between 1906 and 1911. After his death, colleagues compiled under Saussure's name *The Course in General Linguistics,* published in 1915, for which they based themselves on students' notes that were taken down during Saussure's lectures. It is the work of Saussure and the Prague Linguistic Circle that was first labelled **structuralism**: an analytic approach that tries to identify structures and systems in linguistics, literature and poetics. In the 1950s and 1960s we see further penetration of the Saussurian methodology into areas such as anthropology (Claude Levi-Strauss), philosophy, art etc. Before reviewing the literary theories of a few structuralist and post-structuralist critics, we have to familiarize ourselves with Saussure's place in the history of language studies and his concepts.

F. de Saussure. The Russian linguist V. N. Vološinov provides us with proper information about Saussure in his book *Marxism and the Philosophy of Language,* published in 1929. Vološinov describes two basic trends in the philosophy of language: the first he terms 'individualistic subjectivism' and the second 'abstract objectivism'. Vološinov singles out Wilhelm von Humbold as the most important representative of the first trend. 'Humbold exposited his ideas on philosophy

51

of language in his study, *Ueber die Verschiedenheiten des menschlichen Sprachbaues, Gesammelte Werke, VI,* (Berlin, 1841–1852).[1]

Vološinov summarizes individualistic subjectivism's outlook on language into these four basic principles:

1. *Language is activity, an unceasing process of creation (energeia) realized in individual speech acts;*

2. *The laws of language creativity are the laws of individual psychology;*

3. *Creativity of language is meaningful creativity, analogous to creative art;*

4. *Language as a ready-made product (ergon), as a stable system (lexicon, grammar, phonetics), is, so to speak, the inert crust, the hardened lava of language creativity, of which linguistics makes an abstract construct in the interests of the practical teaching of language as a ready-made instrumenta.*[2]

The second trend doesn't really have one founder equal to W. von Humbold; the roots go back to Cartesian [of or relating to the philosopher Descartes] grounds and its ideas were first clearly expressed in Leibniz's conception of universal grammar. When giving a characterization of the modern state (in 1929) of abstract objectivism, Vološinov notes that the ideas of abstract objectivism 'all have been endowed with clarity and precision by Ferdinand de Saussure.'

Volosinov summarizes the outlook of abstract objectivism on language in the following principles:

1. *[a] Language is a stable, immutable system of normatively identical linguistic forms which the individual consciousness finds ready-made and which is incontestable for that consciousness.*

2. *The laws of [a] language are the specifically linguistic laws of connection between linguistic signs within a given, closed linguistic system. These laws are objective with respect to any subjective consciousness.*

3. *Specifically linguistic connections have nothing in common with ideological values (artistic, cognitive or other). Language phenomena are not grounded in ideological motives. No connection of a kind natural and comprehensible to the consciousness or of an artistic kind obtains between the word and its meaning.*

4. *Individual acts of speaking are, from the viewpoint of [a] language, merely fortuitous refractions and variations or plain and simple distortions of normatively identical forms; but precisely these acts of individual discourse*

explain the historical changeability of linguistic forms, a changeability that in itself, from the standpoint of the language system, is irrational and sense-less. There is no connection, no sharing of motives, between the system of [a] language and its history. They are alien to one another.[3]

Saussure's theory departs from the distinction between 'langage' (the universal human phenomenon of language), 'langue' (a specific language, for example French) and 'parole' (language in performance, i.e. specific speech acts). 'Langage', 'langue' and 'parole' are commonly translated as 'language', 'a language' and 'speech acts' or 'speech'. Saussure states that language cannot be the object of linguistic study: 'Language in its entirety has many and different and disparate effects. It is at the same time physical, physiological and psychological. It belongs both to the individual and to society. No classification of human phenomena provides any single place for it, because language as such has no discernible unity.'[4] Saussure expresses the same opinion more strongly in this statement: 'Language in its totality is unknowable for its lack of homogenity.'[5]

Saussure dismisses the idea of taking speech act as the object of linguistic study, because: '…it would be impossible to photograph [to record and visualize] acts of speech in all their details.'[6] Moreover, Saussure considers a language to be social and essential, while he thinks of speech as individual supportive 'and more or less accidental.'[7] What does Saussure identify as the object of linguistic study?

> *The linguist must take the study of linguistic structure as his primary concern, and relate all other manifestations of language to it. Indeed, amid so many dualities, linguistic structure seems to be the one thing that is independently definable and provides something our minds can satisfactorily grasp…*[8]

> *A language as a structured system,…is both a self-contained whole and a principle classification. As soon as we give linguistic structure pride of place among the facts of language, we introduce a natural order into an aggregate which lends itself to no other classification.*[9]

Saussure anchors his study of 'a language as a structured system' within a synchronic frame: 'It is clear that the synchronic point of view takes precedence over the diachronic,

since for the community of language users that is the one and only reality.'[10] Saussure attaches the same 'accidental' nature to diachronic events as he does to speech: 'In spite of appearances to the contrary, diachronic events are always accidental and particular in nature.'[11]

That speech and diachronic events have the same nature follows from the reasoning that speech is the source of diachronic events: "…everything which is diachronic in languages is only so through speech. Speech contains the seeds of every change, each one being pioneered in the first instance by a certain number of individuals before entering into general usage.'[12]

Speech, diachronic events in language and the history of languages don't fit into Saussure's study of a synchronic, logical, structured system of a language. What is the substance of a structured system of a language for Saussure? It's the linguistic sign: 'a two-sided psychological entity,'[13] which can be represented by the following diagrams: (The whole is designated by 'sign'.)

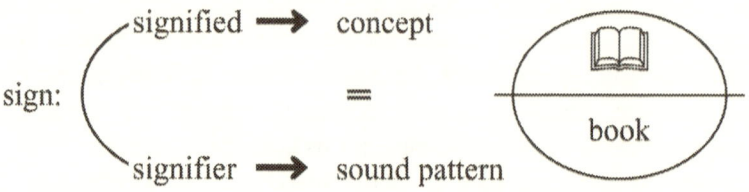

NB Instead of Saussure's picture of a tree, I use the picture of a book.

Words, or in Saussure's terminology 'linguistic signs' have two sides: a sound pattern and a concept. In Saussure's theory, concepts are products of the mind and therefore 'psychological' entities; sound patterns are of psychological nature, too: 'The psychological nature of our sound patterns becomes clear when we consider our linguistic activity. Without moving either lips or tongue, we can talk to ourselves or recite silently a piece of verse. We grasp the words of a language as sound patterns. That's why it is best to avoid referring to them as composed of speech sounds.'[14] Saussure stresses that the link between signifier and signified is arbitrary: 'the linguistic sign is arbitrary.'[15] This idea is expressed—differently—in the following quotations:

> *Languages are not mechanisms created and organised with a view to the concepts to be expressed, although people are mistakenly inclined to think so.*[16]

> *The language itself is a form, not a substance.* [17]

When the link between signifier and signified is arbitrary: how do words take up their meanings? Saussure answers: 'In a sign what matters more than any idea or sound associated with it is what other signs surround it.... A linguistic system is a series of phonetic differences matched with a series of conceptual differences.'[18] More precisely formulated: a sign takes up its meaning through its differentation—phonetical as well as conceptual—from all the other signs.

Providing a critical analysis of Saussure's theory will take us far away from literary theory but I think that it's necessary to mention a few objections. Saussure's distinction between a language—that can be studied—and, language and speech—that cannot be studied—is rejectable because the main ingredient of language is speech. Saussure writes: 'a man who loses the ability to speak none the less retains his grasp of the language system...A language system, as distinct from speech, is an object that may be studied independently. Dead languages are no longer spoken, but we can perfectly well acquaint ourselves with their linguistic structure.'[19] 'Tackling' the man who loses his speaking ability, this man had already formed his consciousness by hearing, speaking, seeing etc. This man's 'grasp of the language system' is based on his use of language—**language made up of speech**. Therefore it's unfair of Saussure to separate speech from 'the language system'.

Through history all languages were spoken by people, and writing has been applied only relatively recently to a number of languages. When disregarding speech as object for linguistic study, it's similarly to studying the capitalist economy without capital! Also, Saussure's argument that we still can study the linguistic structure of dead languages is partly true—though many languages have not been recorded—however, these dead languages, which were once alive, were not made up of visible marks such as letters and hieroglyphs, but made up of human speech. Therefore, this human speech can be only perfectly understood when it's positioned in its social and ideological context. This context, as well as speech and language, don't fit into Saussure's synchronic system which doesn't acknowledge language to be a continuous becoming and changing 'process' that moves along with the ever changing society.

Saussure's concept of the linguistic sign's arbitrariness ought to be supplemented with Saussure's statement that: 'Linguistic signs although essentially psychological, are not abstractions. The associations, ratified by collective agreement, which go to make up the language are realities localised in the brain.'[20] If the link between signifier and signified is arbitrary (as Saussure states), then we need a 'collective agreement' before a linguistic sign in its differentation from the other signs becomes a part of language. In reality, I have never noticed this phenomenon; for example Karl Marx—being a person and not just a sound—signified by his theoretical and political work 'the concept' of Marxism. It's possible to differentiate Marxism from Darwinism, structuralism, barbarism etc., but to understand what Marxism stands for it might be more suitable to study Marx's writings. There's no arbitrariness between the signifier Karl Marx and the signified theory and political praxis of Marxism; and I'm sure of the complete lack of associations and their ratification by collective agreement regarding Marxism.

I still have to remark that reality, instead of Saussure's 'realities', is localised in—and outside the brain; our languages, based in—and outside the brain, are filled with and made up of abstractions from this reality.

V. Shklovsky. One of Russian formalism's leaders, Victor Shklovsky (b. 1893), developed the literary concept of 'defamiliarization: making strange—making different. This concept is essentialy Saussurian: it treats literary technique and form as a system of differentiation. Shklovsky explains:

> *Tolstoy makes the familiar seem strange by not naming the familiar object…In describing something he avoids the accepted names of its parts and instead names corresponding parts of other objects. For example in 'Shame' Tolstoy 'defamiliarizes' the idea of flogging in this way: 'to strip people who have broken the law, to hurl them to the floor, and to rap on their bottoms with switches,'… 'to lash about on the naked buttocks.' Then Tolstoy remarks:*
> **Just why precisely this stupid, savage means of causing pain and not any other—why not prick the shoulders or any part of the body with needles, squeeze the hands or feet in a vise, or anything like that?** [Shklovsky]
> *The familiar act of flogging is made unfamiliar both by the description and by the proposal to change its form without changing its nature.*[21]

It's obvious that Tostoy describes flogging in the first part; in the second part he doesn't describe flogging, but carried on by satanic imagination, he details an act of torture—inflicting intense pain by pricking the shoulders or any part of the body. Tolstoy's abrupt 'descriptive' change from flogging into torture cannot be explained as making flogging 'unfamiliar'. Besides, the nature of flogging is undeniably different from squeezing a person's hand or feet in a vise! Expanding his concept Shklovsky presents 'imagery in erotic art' as a form of 'defamiliarization':

> *Erotic subjects may…be presented figuratively with the obvious purpose of leading us away from their 'recognition.' Hence sexual organs are referred to in terms of lock and key or quilting tools, or bow and arrow, or rings and marlinspikes.*[21]

A writer 'defamiliarizes' when using lock and key instead of sexual organs' proper names but does figurative and defamiliarizing language have an absolute merit over literal language? I will quote some fragments from the Japanese Nobel Prize winner Kenzaburo Oe's novel *A Personal Matter*.

> *Bird walked Himiko home; he grabbed her in the darkness in the lumberyard behind her boarding house. They faced each other in the cold, shivering, and their caresses were simple until Bird's hand, as though by accident, touched Himiko's vagina.... None the less, when he realized he would not be able to insert his penis as long as they were standing, Bird felt humiliated by circumstance, which made him dogged.*[23]

Now I will defamiliarize the sexual organs:

> Bird walked Himiko home; he grabbed her in the darkness in the lumberyard behind her boarding house. They faced each other in the cold, shivering, and their caresses were simple until Bird's hand, as though by accident, touched Himiko's lock.... None the less, when he realized he would not be able to insert his key as long as they were standing, Bird felt humiliated by circumstance, which made him dogged.

It seems that defamiliarization doesn't make much sense in Oe's literature: the context isn't proper for defamiliarization. Anyway, in Shklovsky's differentiating between literal and and figurative language, I don't perceive unique progress since Aristotle's description of the metaphor and simile.

About the purpose of imagery Shklovsky remarks: 'to create a special perception of the object—it creates a vision of the object instead of serving as a means for knowing it.'[23] Literary images such as metaphors (Life is a journey.) and similes (Her face is like a Noh-mask.) create, sometimes, a better understanding —**knowing**—of feelings, actions, experiences and objects in a few words. In ordinary language I would need more words, sentences or paragraphs to convey the knowledge of the foregoing metaphor and simile, and the huge fabric of human experience on which they are based and with which they are interwoven. So much about Victor Shklovsky and his concept of 'defamiliarization'. Let us see how we fare with Roman Jakobson (1896–1982), who is described as 'one of the most powerful minds in twentieth century intellectual history.'[25]

R. Jakobson. His main contribution to literary theory is the identification of discourse along the metaphoric and metonymic poles. He departs from the Saussurian principle that language, like the system of linguistic signs, has a two-fold character: selection and combination. Metaphor depending on the similarity of things (woman and peach), corresponds to the selection axis of language. Metonymy consists of combining an attribute, cause or effect of a thing signifying the same thing (substitute Dostoyevsky for *Crime and Punishment*: Have you read Dostoyevsky?) and thus represents the combination axis of language. Jakobson bases his theory of metaphoric and metonymic poles on aphasia:

> *Every form of aphasic disturbance consists in some impairment, more or less severe, either of the faculty for selection and substitution or for combination and contexture. The former affliction involves a deterioration of metalinguistic operations, while the latter damages the capacity for maintaining the hierarchy of linguistic units. The relation of similarity is suppressed in the former, the relation of contiguity in the latter[,] type of aphasia. Metaphor is alien to the similarity disorder, and metonymy to the contiguity disorder.*[26]

Regarding literature, Jakobson explains:

> *The primacy of the metaphoric process in the literary schools of romanticism and symbolism has been repeatedly acknowledged, but it is still insufficiently realized that it is the predominance of metonymy which underlies and actually predetermines the so-called 'realistic' trend,...*[27]

I strongly doubt the validity of Jakobson's assignment of the metaphoric-metonymic principle' to language and literature for the following two reasons:
1. There's discourse without any metaphoric and metonymic poles:

> *"Jump across the fire to me. Come on! If you jump across the fire to me..." The girl was breathing hard, but her voice came clearly, firmly. The naked boy didn't hesitate an instant. He sprang from tiptoe and his body, shining in the flames, came flying at full speed into the fire. In the next instant he was directly in front of the girl. His chest lightly touched her breasts.*[28]
> [from *The Sound of Waves*, Yukio Mishima]

I cannot imagine how Jakobson would treat the foregoing quotation, which lacks metaphors and metonymies. Also, a writer using the movement enforcements axis such as sound and silence, or a writer giving specific meaning to a phrase using intonation technique, etc., absolutely defies Jakobson's 'metaphoric-metonymic principle'.

2. Although it has been generally accepted in linguistic circles to depart from—and use aphasia as a backbone: in comparison I think it's definitely wrong

to understand and explain the functioning of a healthy body by departing from an analysis of a very ill body. Aphasia is often caused by head-wounds and diseases that injure the brain. Dr. Henry Head recognizes four types of aphasia in wounded soldiers. I'll quote only the first type of aphasia that he describes:

> *Type 1 reacts well to other's people speech, and in milder cases, uses words for the proper objects, but mispronounces or confuses his words; in extreme cases, the sufferer can say little more than 'yes' and 'no'. A patient reports, with some difficulty: "I know it's not......the correct......pronounciation...... I don't always......corret it......because I shouldn't get it right......in five or six times......unless someone says it for me." In a more serious case, the patient, when asked his name, answers Honus instead of 'Thomas,' and says erst for 'first' and hend for 'second.*[29]

When aphasic patients mispronounce words or omit necessary sounds of words, can this be exemplified by a restriction or blocking of the metonymic processes? Is a patient's metaphoric ability suppressed when the patient can't pronounce his name properly? How do patients who only answer with 'yes' or 'no' support Jakobson's theory? How do confusement and mispronounciation from patients with brain disease and malfunctioning speech organs contribute to a literary theory of the metaphoric and metonymic poles?

Concludingly, Jakobson's assignment of the two-fold metaphoric-metonymic character to language is a very meagre contribution to literary theory that cannot even be applied as a principle of literary theory!

L. Bloomfield. In the U.S.A., Leonard Bloomfield (1887–1949), worked out structuralism. Bloomfield combined comparative linguistics. general linguistics and practical language study. However he didn't include literary theory in his extensive linguistic research. Later, structuralism in the U. S. A. was replaced by grammar concentrated theories developed by Noam Chomsky.

Roland Barthes. In the 1950s and 1960s we see further penetration of the Saussurian methodology into the social sciences; anthropology (Claude Levi-Strauss) and literary theory (i.e., Roland Barthes 1915–1980). Barthes is described as 'the most brilliant and influential of the generation of literary critics who came to prominence in France in the 1960s.'[30]

One of Barthes most incredible statements: 'the birth of the reader must be at the cost of the death of the Author,' comes at the end of his famous essay *The Death of the Author*, written in 1968. Barthes starts this essay with quoting a sentence from Balzac's story *Sarrasine*, and asks himself, who the originator is of that sentence. Is it the story's hero? Is it Balzac the writer or Balzac the individual?

Barthes answers: 'we shall never know, for the good reason that writing is the destruction of every voice, of every point of origin. Writing is that neutral, composite, oblique space where our subject slips away, the **negative** where all identity is lost, starting with the very identity of the body writing.'[31] If Barthes truly believes his own naive postulate, then I don't understand why he published his writings under his own name. He should have published anonymously. Writing isn't the destruction of every point of origin. Bakhtin writes:

> *We find the author outside the work as a human being living his own biographical life. But we also meet him (that is, we sense his activity) most of all in the composition of the work: it is he who segments the work into parts...*[32]

How can writing be that 'neutral, composite, oblique space' when a writer's activity can be sensed in the composition of a work; when a writer's personal feelings of hurt and loneliness (compare Y. Kawabata), are processed into his literary work. And a writer might have absorbed a lot of past and present literature, but in the end it's up to the writer's ingenuity to employ different and new axis of movement enforcements; to develop new literary styles and techniques; writing can be that **positive**, where identity—the writer's identity—is found.

In his essay of four pages, Barthes names the following authors: H. Balzac, C. Baudelaire, B. Brecht, G. Flanbert, S. Mallarmé, M. Proust, T. de Quincey and P. Vallery. Still, Barthes writes: 'It is language which speaks, not the author; to write is…, to reach that point where only language acts, "performs" and not 'me'.[33] 'The removal of the Author…is not merely an historical fact or an act of writing; it utterly transforms the modern text (or—which is the same thing—the text is henceforth made and read in such away that at all its levels the author is absent).[34]

Perhaps Barthes doesn't write modern texts because he names many authors. Contrary to Barthes, I think that texts need the 'presence' of their authors. The authors' presence manifests itself from the very beginning of texts—the author choosing a title—until the end, which is decided by the author again. It isn't only language that speaks but the author as well. In art, it is the painter who expresses himself or herself (a chair or sunflower cannot express itself), but Barthes is extreme enough to deny—devalue the necessary link between the genius Vincent van Gogh and his paintings: 'while criticism still consists for the most part in saying that Baudelaire's work is the failure of Baudelaire the man, Van Gogh's his madness,…The explanation of a work is always sought in the man or woman who produced it,…[35] Instead, Barthes insists on the removal of the author and the genius painter when discussing literature and art. It can be assumed that when reflecting on Van Gogh's paintings, Barthes wants us to explain and analyse the dried up, plastered paint on a canvas, while we must cover the **frame** and the painter's signature. At the end of his essay *The Death of the Author*, Barthes stresses the importance of the reader:

> *The reader is the space on which all the quotations that make up a writing are inscribed without any of them being lost; a text unity lies not in its origin but in its destination. Yet this destination cannot any longer be personal; the reader is without history, without biography, psychology; he is simply that someone who holds together in a single field all the traces by which the written text is constituted.*[36]

Barthes proclamation about the 'birth of the reader' doesn't consider that every author is a reader. 'Reader and author' is a unity based on the consumptive and productive natures of the language functions. Before someone becomes an author, he or she has been a reader and while an author writes, he or she reads. When Barthes states that the reader is without history, biography, psycholog: then how about the author who is a reader, too.

The structuralist methodology of identifying and analysing structures that underlie Roland Barthes' approach to the narrative can be labelled anti-human-ist[b], anti-historical[c] and anti-scientific[e]. This labelling can be proved by quoting Barthes' introductory sentence to his textual analysis (1973) of Edgar Allan Poe's story *Valdemar*:

> *To be frank, I ought to add this…we shall not speak of the author, Edgar Poe, nor of the literary history of which he is a part, we shall not take into account the fact that the analysis will be carried out on a translation…*[37]

After Barthes strong statement about not speaking of the author, Edgar Poe etc., he suddenly backs down and states: 'This does not necessarily mean that these problems [the author and the literary history of which he is a part etc.] will not pass into our analysis.'[38] Consequently, Barthes makes up a reason of 'cultural quotations' and 'departures of codes' to justify the reviewing of 'these problems' in his literary analysis. Barthes breaks down Edgar Poe's story into small units, which he calls lexias, and shows how these units convey different meanings according to different codes. These codes can be described like viewpoints, such as cultural, metalinguistic, scientific and ethical viewpoints. Following the analysis of Poe's story, Barthes writes in his methodological conclusions:

We have seen in Poe's story, that one sentence very often refers to two codes simulta-
neously, without one being able to choose which is the 'true' one (for example, the
scientific code and the symbolic code): what is specific to the text, once it attains the
quality of a text, is to constrain us to the undecidability of the codes. In the name of
what could we decide? In the author's name?.... Undecidability is not a weakness,
but a structural condition of narration: there is no unequivocal determination of
the enunciation: in an utterance several codes and several voices are there, without
priority. Writing is precisely this loss of origin, this loss of 'motives' to the profit of a
volume of indeterminations or overdeterminations: this volume is precisely 'signifi-
*ance*ʳ 39

I can follow Barthes' theory about the undecidability of codes; but why should it be necessary to choose one code? It doesn't matter whether several codes are simultaneously present in a sentence, paragraph or story. Sometimes, we can decide in the 'authors name' which codes are present in a text.

Takiji Kobayashi (1903–1933), a Japanese writer and political agitator for the Communist Party (tortured to death by the police), submitted his work *The Factory Ship* with a commentary to the publisher. This commentary gives us the key to several codes:

There are no heroes in this work...[symbolic code], *I have rejected all attempts at*
depicting characters or delving into psychology...[psychological code], [I am]
making my works overwhelmingly proletarian in approach and content...[politi-
cal code], *In this work I have dealt with the unique form of labor found on the*
crab-processing ships, [social-political code], *but this does not mean I have pre-*
pared an exhaustive description of what such a ship is like. [literary style code], *I*
have tried to show (a) that this is a classical example of the exploitation being car-
ried out in the colonies and new Japanese territories; [Marxist code], *(b) that*
when we step outside of the industrialized areas of Tokyo and Osaka, we see that
the present condition of eighty percent of the laborers throughout Japan is exactly
like the conditions that exist in the factory ships; [Marxist code], *and (c) that it*
was a fitting method by which I could clearly (almost transparently) exemplify the
interlocking network of the international web formed by the military and business.
[Leninist code of imperialism] 40

Takiji Kobayashi's comment is a good example of writing with a presence of origin and illuminating motives! In conclusion, Barthes theory is easily refuted and therefore not useful for developing and understanding of literary production and literature.

^{b} Anti-humanist; disregards the conscious, purposive action of Edgar Allan Poe's writing process.

^{c} Anti-historical: Barthes tries to extricate structure from within the text, sacrificing the historical environment surrounding Edgar Allan Poe and his literary work.

^{d} Anti-scientific; Edgar Allan Poe's narrative, written in his mother language, might signify meanings and contexts that disappear in translation.

^{e} "'Signifiance is the without–endness of the possible oprerations in a given field of language…it is through the concept of 'signifiance' that the text becomes erotic…"[41] [Barthes' definition]

Post-structuralism. New literary theories arise in the late 1960s. They are collectively named post-structuralism. Some of post-structuralism's main theorists are Jacques Lacan (1901–1984), Jacques Derrida (1930–) and Michel Foucault (1926–1984).

Jacques Lacan, a French psychoanalyst, approached literature in a Freudian way. For Lacan, the unconsciousness is structured like language and from this viewpoint he starts intermingling psychoanalysis and linguistics. Lacan departs from Saussurian concepts (signifier-signified) which he correctly doubts, but borrows the 'inadequate' metaphoric and metonymic poles from Jakobson.

Lacan identifies[11] the metaphoric pole with Freud's category of condensation^f and the metonymic pole with displacement^g. Since Lacan was more occupied with working out a revitalized Freudian theory than working on a new literary theory, let's turn our attention, very briefly, to **Jacques Derrida**, a French philosopher, whose main contributions are in philosophy and literary studies. J. Derrida is the originator of **deconstruction**: a branch of post-structuralism. A deconstructive reading analyses a text in a sceptical and critical way: exposing contradictions and finding gaps in logical arguments. For Derrida meanings are always different and deferred which leads to the consequences that texts are never simple and unified; texts can't have a determinate meaning. Derrida defines his deconstructive reading method as follows:

> *the reading must always aim at a certain relationship unperceived by the writer, between what he commands and what he does not command of the patterns of the language that he uses. This relationship is not a certain quantitative distribution*

of shadow and light, of weakness or of force, but a signifying structure that critical reading should produce.[42]

When assuming that Derrida's use of 'patterns of language' isn't merely limited to grammatical or linguistic structures but extends also to people's consciousness (Language = consciousness), then Derrida's viewpoint coincides partly with my conclusion that a writer brings unintentional meanings, motives and understandings into his or her literary work. The 'unperceived' in Derrida's definition coincides with my 'unintentional', which establishes a certain degree of agreement between Derrida's and my description about a writer's functioning. However, Derrida wants, subsequently, to compose a 'signifying structure' out of material that is derived from the confrontation between what a writer perceives and what a writer doesn't perceive, which I don't consider a constructive method. After having defined my viewpoint—the reader's viewpoint—it's necessary to expose the writer's unintentional meanings and to frame the writer and his or her literary work in a social-historical context whereupon we can recognize a unified text with a determinate meaning. Not considering Derrida's deconstruction of philosophy, anthropology and linguistics (because these fields of inquiry fall outside the scope of literary theory): I think that Derrida's method of deconstructive reading is an inadequate tool for literary theory because of its preposed assumption of the writer's perception (what does a writer see and what doesn't a writer see) and this 'perception' isn't incorporated—as it ought to have been—into the deconstructive reading process itself.

---

[f] Condensation is the process by which one element in a dream may represent more than one dream-thought and refer to more than one event, anxiety etc., in the dreamers waking life.[43]

[g] Displacement refers to the way a dream is often differently centred from the preoccupations which give rise to it, a trivial event in reality being of prime importance in the dream.[44]

Michel Foucault didn't consider himself a literary critic, 'I'm not a literary critic nor a literary historian.'[45] In 1984, at the time of his death, he was a Professor of the History of Systems of Thought. In reaction to the effort of modern criticism to abolish the author as the owner of the language that speaks in his text (not the writer, but only language acts and performs according to Barthes), it was

Michel Foucault who restored, temporarily[h] the place and function of the author. Foucault states:

> an author's name is not simply an element in a discourse…it performs a certain classifactory function. Such a name permits one to group together a certain number of texts, define them, differentiate them from and contrast them to others. In addition it establishes a relationship among the texts…The author's name serves to characterize a certain mode of being of discourse: the fact that the discourse has an author's name,…shows that discourse is not an ordinary every day speech that merely comes and goes, not something that is immediately consumable. On the contrary, it is a speech that must be received in a certain mode and that, in a given culture, must receive a certain status.[46]

After this passage Foucault analyses this 'author-function' from a historical viewpoint in connection with the different types of discourse, such as scientific, religious and literary discourses. Foucault's remark that a discourse is 'not something immediately consumable' contradicts my description of pure passive reading, sometimes, people consume literature as fast food. Foucault, who acknowledges the function of the author's name in the foregoing quotation, expresses a very different opinion about author and reader in a discussion for the Italian weekly Panorama, in April 1984 (three months before his death).

> **Allesandro Fontana:** It is a fact that, although there may still be good authors, there are fewer and fewer good readers.
> **M. Foucault:** Never mind "good" readers—I'd say fewer and fewer readers. And it's true one isn't read anymore. One's first book is read, because one isn't known, because people don't know who one is, and it is read in disorder and confusion, which suits me fine…. It doesn't bother me particularly if a book, given that it is read, is read in different ways. What is serious is that, as one goes on writing books, one is no longer read at all, and from distortion to distortion, reading out of others' readings, one ends up with an absolutely grotesque image of the book. This does indeed pose a problem: is one to involve oneself in polemics and reply to each of these distortions…or leave the book to be distorted to the point at which it becomes a caricature of itself,…?

---

[h] At the end of his essay, Foucault foresees the possibility that with our changing society, the author-function will disappear. [47]

For Foucault it's already obvious that one can't expect to find 'good' readers. Critics, authors, readers etc. are reading in 'disorder' and 'confusion': creating 'distortion' to 'distortion'. Though Foucault speaks about his own scientific books,

we may safely assume that literary texts are included in Foucault's scope because he groups history of ideas, knowledge, literature, philosophy and the sciences, together under the notion of 'author' in his essay *What is an Author?* How can Foucault's ideas that an author's discourse isn't 'immediately consumable', 'must receive a certain status' etc., be brought in accordance with the reality of 'no longer read at all' and, 'books ending up as caricatures of themselves?' If books are no longer being read it means they aren't consumed at all. If the author Foucault is pleased with his first book being read in confusion and disorder, he oughtn't be displeased when his next books end up distorted.

I ascribe the discordancy of Foucault's ideas to a discrepancy between his scientific interpretation and his personal experience as an author. Taken together, Foucault, the author of scientific texts, shows the same deep desire for being read in a truthful way as the writer O. Dazai expected from literary critics. In the story *Handsome Devils and Cigarettes*, published in March 1948, Dazai writes:

> *Yesterday I was drinking cheap liquor in a bar, when three elderly men of letters came in. Though I was completely not acquainted with them, suddenly, they crowded around me and, in a horrible disorderly drunken manner, totally ignorant of my novels, they spoke ill of my work.*[48]

Dazai singles out the men of letters while Foucault doesn't mention philosophers, historians etc. (his colleagues), but speaks about the readers in general. In a straightforward way, Dazai tackles literary criticism in his short stories; Foucault speaks out against his critics (probably his colleagues and commentators), in interviews.

In the essay *What is an Author*, Foucault describes the appearance of a new type of author in the nineteenth century:

> *there appeared in Europe another, more uncommon, kind of author, whom one should confuse with neither the 'great' literary authors, nor the authors of religious texts, nor the founders of science. In a somewhat arbitrary way we shall call those who belong to this last group 'founders of discursivity.' They are unique in that they are not just the authors of their own works. They have produced something else; the possibilities and rules for the formation of other texts. In this sense, they are very different, for example, from a novelist, who is, in fact nothing more than the*

author of his own text. Freud is not just the author of The interpretations of Dreams or Jokes and their relation to the Unconsciousness; Marx is not just the author of the Communist Manifesto or Capital: they both have established an endless possibility of discourse...., when I speak of Marx or Freud as founders of discursivity, I mean that they made possible not only a certain number of analogies, but also (and equally important) a certain number of differences.[49]

First I have to remark that *Communist Manifesto* appeared under the names of both Marx and Engels. A number of the *Manifesto's* ideas and formulations were previously written by Engels alone. Foucault's distinction between 'founders of discursivity' and, for example novelists, is difficult for me to ascertain. In the film *Crime and Dismeanors* made by Woody Allen, a planned murder of a woman causes anguish to the doctor who requested this murder of his ex-lover. Gradually the doctor regains his mental strength and at the end of the film he emerges as a victor who could 'defeat' his Jewish upbringing, personal feelings of guilt, avoid society's punishment etc. This film's story and Dostoyevsky's *Crime and Punishment* have the same theme of crime and several motifs such as dreams about childhood, confessions, fits of anger and the habit of monologues, in common. After the crimes in the film and novel have been committed, the film's plot develops—although by the same anguish—in an opposite direction from the novel's plot. Thus we can find a number of analogies (premeditated murder, anguish, guilt, etc.) and several differences (defeating Jewish upbringing—giving over to childhood's moral, keeping the murder secret—confession, victory—defeat). Knowing that Woody Allen refers to Dostoyevsky's novels in his films; that he has been influenced by Dostoyevsky's literature in writing his scripts; might we conclude that the novelist Dostoyevsky is a founder of discursivity, too?

As we have briefly reviewed 'contributions' of some literary theorists, a psychoanalyst, a philosopher and a historian; I have to conclude this chapter on the sad note that none of them could lay bare fundamental mechanisms of literary production and literature.

In addition, my critical review of Derrida's concept that "texts are never simple and unified" contrasted sharply with *The Izu Dancer's* Analysis (*See* Chapter 2, Part 1), which induces me to formulate this **constructive** reading method:

By exposing unintentional meanings, motives and understandings that a writer brings into his or her literary work; defining my viewpoint; exposing the writer's viewpoint; framing the writer and his or her literary work in a social—historical context, we can recognize a unified text with a determinate meaning.

NOTES

1. V. N. Vološinov, *Marxism and the Philosophy of Language,* translated by Ladislav Matejka and I. R. Titunik, Cambridge, Massachusetts and London, Harvard University Press, fifth printing 1993, p. 49.

2. Ibid., p. 48.

3. Ibid., p. 57.

4. Ferdinand de Saussure, *Course in* General *Linguistics,* Translated and Annonated by Roy Harris, Chicago and La Salle, Illinois, Open Court, ninth printing 1997, p. 10.

5. Ibid., p. 20.

6. Ibid., p. 15.

7. Ibid., pp. 13–14.

8. Ibid., p. 9.

9. Ibid., p. 10.

10. Ibid., p. 89.

11. Ibid., p. 92.

12. Ibid., pp. 96–97.

13. Ibid., p. 66.

14. Ibid., p. 66.

15. Ibid., p. 67.

16. Ibid., p. 85.

17. Ibid., p. 120.

18. Ibid., p. 118.

19. Ibid., p. 14.

20. Ibid., p. 15.

21. Victor Shklovsky, *Art as technique,* translated by Lee T. Lemon and Marion J. Reis. *Modern Criticism and Theory,* edited by David Lodge, London and New York, Longman, 1988, p. 21.

22. Ibid., p. 25.

23. Kenzaburo Oe, *A Personal Matter,* translated by John Nathan, Tokyo, Charles E. Tuttle Company, eleventh printing 1994.

24. Victor Shklovsky, *Art as technique*, p. 25.

25. Roman Jakobson, *The metaphoric and metonymic poles, Modern Criticism and Theory,* edited by David Lodge, London and New York, Longman, 1988, p. 58.

26. Ibid., pp. 57–58.

27. Ibid., p. 58.

28. Yukio Mishima, *The Sound of Waves,* translated by Meredith Weatherby, Tokyo, Charles E. Tuttle Company, thirtieth printing 1994, p. 76.

29. Leonard Bloomfield, *Language*, originally published in 1933 renewed in 1961 by Leonard Bloomfield. Chicago, The University of Chicago Press, 1984, p. 35.

30. David Lodge, Introduction to Roland Barthes, *Modern Criticism and Theory,* London and New York, Longman, 1988, p. 166.

31. Ibid., Roland Barthes, *The death of the author*, p. 168.

32. M. M. Bakhtin, *The Dialogic Imagination*, edited by Michael Holquist, translated by Caryl Emmerson and Michael Holquist, U. S. A., Austin, University of Texass Press, 1981, p. 254.

33. Roland Barthes, *The death of the author, Modern Criticism and Theory*, edited by David Lodge, London and New York, Longman, 1988, p. 168.

34. Ibid., p. 169.

35. Ibid., p. 168.

36. Ibid., p. 171.

37. Roland Barthes, *Textual Analysis, Untying the Text, A Post–Structuralist Reader,* edited by Robert Young, London and New York, Routledge, reprint 1990, p. 137.

38. Ibid., pp. 137–138.

39. Ibid., p. 158.

40. Takiji Kobayashi, *"The Factory Ship" and "The Absentee Landlord"*, translated by Frank Motofuji, U. S. A., University of Washington Press, 1973, p. X VIII.

41. Roland Barthes, *Theory of the Text, Untying the Text, A Post–Structuralist Reader*, edited by Robert Young, London and New York, Routledge, reprint 1990, p. 38.

42. Jacques Derrida, *Of Grammatology*, translated by Gayatri Chakravorty Spivak, Baltimore and London, The John Hopkins University Press, 1997, p. 158.

43. David Lodge, *Modern Criticism and Theory*, editor's footnote at J. Lacan's essay *The insistence of the letter in the unconsciousness*, London and New York, Longman, 1988, p. 92.

44. Ibid., p. 92.

45. Michel Foucault, *Death and the Labyrinth, The world of Raymond Roussel*, translated by Charles Ruas, Postsript, *An Interview with Michel Foucault by Charles Ruas*, London, The Athlone Press, 1987, p. 184.

46. Michel Foucault, *What is an author?*, *Modern Criticism and Theory*, edited by David Lodge, London and New York, Longman, 1988, p. 201.

47. Michel Foucault, *Politics, Philosophy, Culture, Interviews and other writings 1977–1984*, edited by Lawrence D. Kritzman, London and New York, Routledge, 1990, p. 52.

48. Osamu Dazai, *Bidanshi to Tabako, Shayo–Ningen Shikkaku*, Tokyo, Shinchosha, 1979, p. 319, translated by W. Nuyten.

49. Michel Foucault, *What is an author?*, *Modern Criticism and Theory*, edited by David Lodge, London and New York, Longman, 1988, p. 206.

2

Mikhail Mikhailovich Bakhtin

Bakhtin (1895–1975) finished St. Petersburg University in 1918, where he had studied classics. He considered himself essentially a philosopher and not a literary critic. He started his work as a teacher and writer during the years of revolution and civil war in Russia. In 1919, Bakhtin published a small work called *Art and Responsibility,* which was a brief summary for a major work on moral philosophy which only got published in 1979 (four years after Bakhtin died). In 1921, Bakhtin married E. A. Okolovic, who supported him until she died in 1971.

In 1924, Bakhtin started to work at the Historical Institute and consulted for the State Publishing House in Leningrad. Very often Bakhtin's manuscripts were suppressed or lost, by chance or by the oppostion of enemies. This is one of the likely reasons that Bakhtin published three books *Freudianism* (1927), *Marxism and the Philosophy of Language* (1929) and *The Formal Method in Literary Scholarship* (1928) under the names of his friends V.N. Vološinov and P.N. Medvedev. Right after Bakhtin's work *Problems of Dostoevsky's Art* (1929) was published, he was sent into exile in Kazakhstan, where he had to work as a bookkeeper for the next six years. During this period, his friends at the libraries of Moscow and Leningrad, continued supplying Bakhtin with books needed for his studies.

In 1937, Bakhtin moved back to Kimry, a town two hundred kilometers from Moscow, where he finished a manuscript on the eighteenth-century German novel. Publishers lost this manuscript in the confusion of the German invasion and Bakhtin used the only other copy of this manuscript to roll his cigarettes! Around the same time, they amputated Bakhtin's leg because of a bone disease that had started in 1923. During World War II, Bakhtin lived in Moscow, and in 1940 he submitted a dissertation on Rabelais, which he could defend only after the war. The defence wasn't successful: after several stormy meetings between officials who were appointed to preside over the defence of Bakhtin's dissertation and opposing professors, the State Accrediting Bureau denied Bakhtin his doctorate in 1949. The dissertation *Rabelais and Folk Culture of the Middle Ages and*

Renaissance, was published in 1965. In the meantime, Bakhtin had become the head of the Department of Russian and World Literature at the University in Saransk (1957), a place where he had taught in 1936. Bakhtin had to give up his teaching position in 1961 due to declining health. In 1969, he returned to Moscow, where he lived until his death in 1975.

Distinguishing The Novel During the 1930s Bakhtin wrote four essays about the theory of the novel, which originally appeared in *Voprosy literatury I este iki* (Moscow 1975). They were published in their English version in the *Dialogic Imagination* (1981).[1] The first essay entitled *Epic and Novel*, starts with the observation that developing a theory of the novel is extremely difficult because the novel as a genre is still in development while other genres are already 'completed and in part already dead.' Comparing the novel with other genres, Bakhtin gives the following basic principles that distinguish the novel from other genres:

> *(1) its* [the novel's] *stylistic three-dimensionality which is linked with the multi-languaged consciousness realized in the novel; (2) the radical change it effects in the temporal coordinates of the literary image; (3) the new zone opened by the novel for structuring literary images, namely, the zone of maximal contact with the present (with contemporary reality) in all its openendedness.*[2]

Referring to the first basic principle, Bakhtin describes how polyglossia[a] even existed before pure canonic monoglossia, however, works produced by the Classical Greeks, for example, were the result of a creative consciousness that resided in closed, pure languages. Polyglossia was used (tragedy is a polyglot genre) but languages and dialects coexisted as independent entities. From the Greek literary language Bakhtin extracts 'the struggle for the unity of a literary language and for the unity of its systems of genres.'[3] Opposingly, in the modern European novel (seventeenth century), Bakhtin sees: 'the struggle between two tendencies in the languages of European people: one a centralizing (unifying) tendency, the other a decentralizing tendency (that is, one that stratifies languages).'

Bakhtin builds up his theory in reference to an immense number of texts and writers. He uses traditional accounts to produce his theory of the novel. While describing and analysing Bakhtin's theory, we might find useful insights, perspectives and materials to establish a theory about the mechanisms of literary production and literature. The struggle of centralising and decentralising tendencies in the languages of European people, which gave birth to a multi-languaged consciousness, is for Bakhtin one of the fundamental points of departure for the modern novel. The **temporal coordinates** of the literary image that Bakhtin specifies for the modern novel (in contrast to the epic), consist of 'portraying an event on the same time-and-value plane as oneself and one's contemporaries (and an event that is therefore based on personal experience and thought.'[5]

The third basic principle Bakhtin gives to distinguish the novel from other genres—**the new zone opened by the novel**—brings the novel into contact with 'extra literary genres': the novel comes into contact with everyday life, with the domains of philosophy, politics, religion etc. 'After' having used these different sources, the novel then degenerates, 'into the raw spirituality of a confession, a "cry of the soul" that has not yet found its formal contours.'[6] The non-existence of formal contours is a distinctive characteristic of the novel being in development.

Having distinguished the novel from epic and other genres in *Epic and Novel*, Bakhtin identifies a number of ancient Greek, Roman and medieval texts that contain embrionic cells of the modern novel. In his essay *From the Prehistory of Novelistic Discourse*, Bakhtin points out the parodying and travestying word in the different genres such as parodic poems, tragedies, comedy, satire etc., that created a distance between language and reality: 'the creating artist began to look at language from the outside, with another's eyes, from the point of view of a potentially different language and style. It's after all, precisely in the light of another potential language or style that a given straightforward style is parodied, travestied, ridiculed.'[7] It's the parodying and travestying word; the culture of laughter, that hand in hand, with polyglossia prepared the ground for the modern novel.

The Chronotope—The Rogue, Clown and Fool—In his third essay *Forms of Time and of the Chronotope in the Novel*, Bakhtin describes various chronotopes[b,] whose 'temporal and spatial determinations are inseperable from one another, and always colored by emotions and value.'[8] Bakhtin distinguishes the various literary genres and their development by
differently functioning of chronotopes. Against this background he treats 'The Greek Romance', 'The Adventure Novel of Every Day Life', 'The Biographical Novel', 'The Chivalric Romance', Rabelais' novel *Gargantua and Pantagruel* and the modern novel.

---

[a] Polyglossia: the simultaneous presence of two or more national languages interacting within a single cultural system.

The chronotope in the ancient Greek novel functions like an alien world in adventure-time. The Greek adventure-time is 'an extra temporal hiatus' between two moments: the beginning, when the the hero and heroine meet each other for the first time—followed by many adventures—and the end of the novel, when the hero and heroine are successfully united in marriage. The adventures (between the beginning and end) such as abduction of the heroine, escape, pursuit, seperation of the hero and heroine, shipwreck, rescue, the hero and heroine being united etc.; take place in an abstract expanse of space: escape to different countries; shipwrecks on the seas; rescues in strange countries; in an alien world.

The link between space and time is only purely technical of nature; for the story it doesn't matter on which sea the shipwreck happens; for escape a person has to go to a different country but for the Greek novel it's not important, in geographical and historical sense, which country is chosen. The hero can escape to Egypt, Babylon or elsewhere. The Greek novel is characterized by this interchangeability of space and the unfolding of the adventures according to adventuristic time—suddenly, just at that moment—that doesn't coincide with real biographical time. The heroes are unchanged, the same age, the same passion, at the beginning and the end of the novel. The time that would have been required to pass through all those adventures is unaccounted for in real time.

The mixture (not mechanical) of adventure-time with everyday-time as exemplified in the novel 'The Golden Ass' is the the second type of chronotope. Three images of Lucius, the main character, fill the plot: Lucius before his transformation into an ass, Lucius while being an ass (metamorphosis) and Lucius' rebirth as a man. After Lucius passed through these 'initiations he enters upon his biographical life as a rethorican and a priest…It's not the time of a Greek romance, a time that leaves no traces. On the contrary, it leaves a deep and irradicable mark on the man himself as well on his entire life. It is nevertheless, decidedly adventure-time: a time of exceptional and unusual events, events determined by chance…' [10] This adventure time is reinforced by the metaphor 'the path of life' and the chronotope of the road. The course of a person's life intertwined with the actual spatial course of the road. Space—the road—gets concrete meanings: the hero and his fate along the road—meetings, escapes, separation—create a concrete chronotopic significance (this in contrast to the Greek roman). Bakhtin stresses the importance of Lucius' metamorphosis into an ass: while passing through life, the ass cannot really be a part of everyday life, but it can study and observe all the secrets of human life. The ass as the 'third-person' can be found in the later history of the novel in the character of the servant, the rogue, the adventurer, the prostitute and the parvenu.

In the genre of Ancient Biography and Autobiography, Bakhtin notes the existence of two types of autobiography in Classical Greece. The first type he calls

'Platonic' because it finds its best expression in the works of Plato. At the heart of this type 'lies the chronotope of the 'life course of one seeking true knowledge.'[11] It's characterized by the dissolution of real time into the ideal time of metamorphosis. The second type of autobiography (and biography), originates from the civic funeral and memorial speech. The internal chronotope of this type isn't so important as the real-life chronotope of the public square where one's own or another's life is exposed to the last detail in public.

---

[b] Chronotope: literally, 'time-space'. A unit of analysis for studying texts according to the ratio and nature of the temporal adventure-time is the most abstract and static of This chronotope of the alien world in all chronotopes. and spatial categories represented.[9]

Only later (Hellenistic and and Roman Era) did the question arise whether glorifying oneself as another person was permissible. The very posing of such a question is evidence that the classical public wholeness of an individual had broken down, and a differentation between biographical and autobiographical forms had begun'[12] This leads to the first real Greek autobiography of Isocratus, followed by the Roman autobiographies. The Roman patrician family, which fused directly with the state—state functions entrusted to the heads of families—approached autobiography from a self-consciousness that 'felt itself to be primarily a link between, on the one hand, deceased ancestors, and on the other, descendants who had not yet entered public life.'[13] Still, the individual's life forms a complete whole with the state (public life).

Bakhtin pays brief attention to the genre of the 'Chivalric Romance' because it functions with adventure-time of the bassically Greek type and the position of space is also only technical of nature. The heroes (in contrast to the Greek romance) are individualized, but at the same time, are symbolic.

The unique, authentic individual that plays an important role in the modern novel, appears on stage in the Renaissance. Characters of the rogue, clown and fool, will transform the ancient novel. Before their concrete appearance, its the **Rabelaisian chronotope** that will 'purge the spatial and temporal world of those remnants of a transcedent worldview still present in it, to clean away symbolic and hierarchical interpretations...'[14] How does Francois Rabelais (c. 1494–1553) work this out methodologically in his novel *Gargantua and Pantagruel*?

The essence of his method consists first of all, in the destruction of all ordinary ties,
of all the habitual matrices of things and ideas, and the creation of unexpected con-

nections, including the most suprising logical links ('alogisms') and linguistic con-
nections (Rabelais' specific etymology, morphology and syntax).[15]

Rabelais uses the clown, rogue and fool, to destroy the old picture of the world and directly interwoven with this destruction of the old, is the construction of a new world for which he relies, 'upon folklore and antiquity—where the contiguity of objects more exactly corresponded to their various natures.' [16]

Rabelais was able to put together or take anything apart by constructing and intersecting the following series (themes): '(1) series of the human body, in its anatomical and physiological aspects; (2) human clothing series; (3) food series;(4) drink and drunkeness series; (5) sexual series (6) death series;(7) defecation series.' [17] The Rabelaisian chronotope can be briefly described as bringing the world into physical contact with the human body. Man (human body) gets a new place in the real spatial-temporal world. Rabelais exposed the coherent, external man, but his characters don't have any internal dialogue. With the transformation of the rogue, clown and fool into major characters in the novel, especially when one of these characters becomes the bearer of the authorial point of view, we arrive at the birth-place of the modern novel, Daniel Defoe (*Moll Flanders*), Jonathan Swift (*Gulliver's Travels*).

In the later part of his essay, Bakhtin mentions and treats the following chronotopes: the castle; parlors and salons (especially important for dialogues); the provincial town; the threshold and related chronotopes such as the street, square, staircase, front hall (extensively used by Dostoyevsky); nature; family-idyllic chronotope and the chronotope of labor-idyll. Bakhtin poses himself the question: 'What is the significance of all these chronotopes?'[18] His immediate answer: 'They are the organizing centers for the fundamental narrative events of the novel. The chronotope is the place where the knots of narrative are tied and untied...to them belongs the meaning that shape narative.' [19]

In his conclusion, Bakhtin adds: 'Science, art, literature also involve semantic elements that are not subject to temporal and spatial determinations...Meanings exist in artistic thought as well...These artistic meanings are likewise not subject to temporal and spatial determinations.' [20] This additional statement makes it clear that the category of chronotope (time-space) has its limitations; semantic elements and artistic meanings exist that aren't affected—covered by temporal and spatial determinations. This is exactly the place, to emphasize the importance of movement enforcements such as 'sound–silence', 'darkness–brightness', 'intonation'—which can be considered to be fundamental organizing centers for the structure of novels.

In conclusion, Bakhtin's work produces very useful insights and concepts about the history of literary production: the concept of a multi-languaged consciousness; the double natured mechanism of time-and-value when portraying events; 'cry of the soul'; the position and functioning of the rogue, clown and fool; and the numerous chronotopes. I will have to carefully observe these insights and concepts in developing this dissertation further.

NOTES

1. M.M. Bakhtin, *The Dialogic Imagination*, Edited by Michael Holquist, trans. Caryl Emmerson and Michael Holquist, Austin, U.S.A., University of Texas Press, 1981.

2. Ibid., *Epic and Novel*, p. 11.

3. Ibid., *From the Prehistory of Novelistic Discourse*, p. 66.

4. Ibid., p. 66.

5. Ibid., p. 14.

6. Ibid., p. 33.

7. Ibid., p. 60.

8. Ibid., *Forms of Time and Chronotope in the Novel*, p. 243.

9. Ibid., Glossary, p. 425.

10. Ibid., *Forms of Time and Chronotope in the Novel*, p. 116.

11. Ibid., p. 130.

12. Ibid., p. 133.

13. Ibid., p. 138

14. Ibid., p. 168

15. Ibid., p. 169.

16. Ibid., p. 170.

17. Ibid., p. 170.

18. Ibid., p. 250.

19. Ibid., p. 250.

20. Ibid., p. 257

21. Ibid., p. 84.

3

A Literary Analysis

In this chapter I will analyze, trying to understand and explain literary mechanisms at work in Ihara Saikaku's short story *Chokyu no Edotana-Everlasting Edo Stores*[1] (Edo is Tokyo's former name). Although a short story isn't exactly the same as a novel, I consider the short story as a literary genre that is directly interwoven with the novel; it's a brief prose novel.

Saikaku (1642–1693), was born to an Osaka merchant family. Working as a merchant, Saikaku wrote haiku (17-syllable poems) in his spare time, until his early thirties. Saikaku's wife passed away in 1675 at the age of twenty-five, leaving Saikaku with three children. Soon after his wife's death, Saikaku shaved off his hair, donned Buddhist priest robes and retired from the merchant world. He started making a living writing and teaching haiku; later he started writing novels.

Everlasting Edo Stores is the last of a collection of twenty stories describing New Year's Eve; the year's financial settlement day, on which lenders tried to recover money they lent and borrowers tried to find ways to avoid paying their debts. The story contents mainly describe people's experiences on how they managed financial affairs on this last, financially important, day of the year. All twenty stories (except *Everlasting Edo Stores*) have dialogues, although these dialogues mainly describe characters' personalities and don't build up the story's narrative structure. Saikaku stages various nameless characters—'son,' 'husband,' 'wife,' etc.—in the stories, but *Everlasting Edo Stores* doesn't have a single character. In this story, Saikaku describes how various **classes** of samurais, servants, craftsmen, store owners and merchants are involved in earning and spending money on New Year's Eve. Descriptions of diverse mercenary activities are interwoven with splendid scenery descriptions and humorous information about rising prices on New Year's Eve.

Saikaku wrote this story in 1691 (two years before his death) in Japanese language, which in terms of pronunciation, grammar and characters, differs greatly from modern Japanese: even for Japanese people, it might look like a puzzle. Therefore, I will first give the original printed version, then my interpretation in modern

Japanese, followed by my English translation. I will mark the **original version o.v.** and page number **p.**—similarly, I will mark the **modern interpretation m.i.** and page number **p.** Notes in the Japanese modern interpretation are taken over in the English translation and explained in English footnotes.

長久の江戸棚

天下泰平、国土万人、江戸商ひを心がけ、其道々の棚出して、諸国より荷物、舩路、岡付の馬かた、毎日数万駄の間屋づき、ことを見れば、世界は金銀たくさんなるものなるに、これをもうくる才覚のならぬは、諸商人に生れて口おしき事ぞかし。

さるほどに、十二月十五日より、通り町のはんじやう、世に賞の市とは爰の事なるべし。常のうりもの棚は捨置て正月のけしき、京羽子板、玉ぶりく、細工に金銀をちりばめ、はま弓一挺を小判二両などにも買人有けるは、緒大名の子息かにぎらず、町人までも万に大気なるゆゑぞかし。町ずじに中棚を出して、商ひにいとまなく、銭は水のごとくながれ、白かねは霰のごとし。

富士の山かげゆたかに、日本橋の人足、百千万の車のとゞろくに鱗なしたり。舩町の魚市、毎朝の賣帳、四方の海ながら、浦々に鱗のたねも有事よと沙汰し侍る。神田須田町の八百屋もの、毎日の大根、里馬に付つゞきて、数万駄見えけるは、とかく畠のありくがごとし。半切にうつしならべたる唐がらしは、秋らかき竜田山をむさし野に見るに似たり。瀬戸物町、糀町の雁鳥さながら、雲の黒きを地にはへたるがごとし。本町の呉服もの、五色の京染、屋しき模やうのちらしがた、四季一度にながめ、すがた山く〳〵、夕べには香ぞかし。傳馬町のつみ綿、見よしの〻雪のあけぼのはなの色香ぞかし。道明らかう、大晦日の夜に入て、二夜千金、家〴〵の大商ひ。殊に、足袋、雪踏は、諸職人、万事買物のおさめにして、夜の明がたに調へに来たり。一とせ、江戸中の棚に、せきだか一足、たびか片足ない事有。

幾万人はけばとて、かゝる事は、日本才一人のあつまり所なれば也。宵のほどは、一そく七八分のせきだ、夜半過には壹匁二三分となり、夜明がたには二そく武匁五分になれ共、買人ばかりにしてうるものなし。一とせ、掛小鯛、二枚十八匁宛せし事も有。

代々ひとつ金子武歩づ〳〵せしに、高ふて買ぬといふ事なし。京大坂にては、相場ちがひのものは、たと〻祝儀のものにしてから、中〳〵調ふべき人心にはあらず。愛を以て大名気とはいへり。京大坂に住なれて、心のちいさきものも、よむといふ事なし。小判をりんゐめにてかける事なし、とれば、又其まゝにさきへわたし、世は廻り持のたからなれば、ひとりとして、吟味する事にはあらず。十七八日までに、上方への銀飛脚の宿を見しに、大分の金銀、色々かはらず上りては、くだり、一とせに道中を幾たびか、金銀ほど世に辛労いたすものは外になし。是ほど世に多きものなれとも、小判一両もたずに、江戸にも年をとるもの有。

されば歳暮の御使者とて、太刀目録、御小袖、樽さかな、箱入のらうそく、何を見ても万代の春めく、町並の門松、これぞちとせ山の山口、なを常盤橋の朝日かげ、豊かに静かに万民の身に照そひ、くもらぬ春にあへり。

Everlasting Edo Stores

Peace reigns over our land. Among our nation's people are Edo store owners trying to do business. Every day, millions of kilograms[1] of produce from all prefectures are delivered to wholesale stores by searoute and cart-horse[2] drivers going over land routes. Observing society overflowing with money, it must be mortifying for people who are born as merchants, but not having the wits to make profit.

In Nihonbashi Toori Quarter, also called 'The Town of Treasure,' trade really prospers from 15 December.[3] People don't pay attention to stores selling reular goods because it's the important business season for selling New Year's articles. Battledores[4] and decorated toys[5] for driving out evil spirits are skillfully decorated with gold and silver foils. Edo's citizens are very liberal-minded considering that not only samuarais, but also tradesmen and craftsmen buy their sons arrow sets[6] for two gold coins apiece.

While street stalls continue business without a break, silver coins whirl and pile up like snow; money streams in like water. Mount. Fuji's figure is dignified; the footsteps of people passing through Nihonbashi Quarter sound like the rumbling of countless carriages. Every morning, the amounts of money written into sales ledgers in Funa Quarter's fish market are amazing. It's often rumored that there are many sorts of fishes in the seas surrounding Japan. Every day, like fields moving in on foot, pack-horses transport millions of kilograms of raddishes to the vegetable market in Kansudo Quarter. Seeing sorted red peppers in shallow buckets[7] is like watching Mount Tatsu's[8] fall colors in Musashino Quarter.

Wild geese and ducks spread like dark clouds all over the place in Setomono and Koji Quarters. Dry-goods stores and samurai mansions in Hon Quarter are decorated with five colored Kyoto dyed drapery.[9] This drapery can be seen only once in the four seasons and suggests a beautiful woman's charm. Cotton piles in front of merchants stores in Denma Quarter look like snow covering the mountains of Yoshino Town at dawn. In the evening, lined up paper lanterns brightly illuminate the streets.

The onset of New Year Eve's night is the beginning of a big golden business night for many households. Towards daybreak, craftsmen are still going to buy their postponed purchase of especially Japanese socks and bamboo sandals.[10] Although a lot of people put on footwear, it would be rare for all footwear to be sold out; but one year, not even a pair of bamboo sandals or a single Japanese sock was left over in Edo's stores; that's why Edo is the most crowded place in Japan. Another time, in the early evening a pair of bamboo sandals went for seven silver coins; after midnight the price went up to twelve silver coins, and reached twenty-five silver coins by daybreak; no sellers were left, only buyers. Another year, a pair of small, salted fish[11] would cost two and a half gold coins, and a New Year's decorative mandarin orange would cost one silver coin, and these products were sold despite their expensive prices.

In Kyoto and Osaka, people hesitate to buy expensive congratulory gifts, but true-born Edoites, with samurais' liberal-minded disposition, buy readily regardless of price. Once people used to Kyoto and Osaka economical life-style move to Edo, they become more easygoing: they stop counting every single coin and weighing gold coins for a triffle. When receiving a small gold coin, people don't look at it carefully and spend it instantly because money is society's circulating wealth.

Watching the inns where money transporting agents stay during their customary visits to Kyoto and vicinity, around 17–18 December, we can see that their money (gold and silver) didn't change its color at all after having come and gone over the Tokai Road many times a year. Nothing else in the world toils as hard as money. Although there is so much money in the world, some people in Edo have less than one gold coin to start the New Year.

Finally, samurais' year-end gift messengers, who seeing all the lists of long swords, kimonos, barrels of wine, boxes of candles, boxes with fish and chicken, observe an everlasting flourishing New Year. Streets decorated with pine boughs remind of the foot of Mount Chitose.[12] The morning sun rays shining on Tokiwa Bridge reflect abundantly and tranquilly on everybody. People welcome a cloudless New Year.

Notes

1. (一) (駄) Horseload unit estimated at 150 kilograms.
2. (二) Cart-horse driver.
3. (三) 15 December in the original text is a mistake. In Nihonbashi Tori Quarter stalls were temporaly set up to sell New Year's decorations from 25 to30 December.
4. (四) Battledore a child's primer made of two or three pages of stiff cardboard on which court officials and the imperial family's ladies were painted.
5. (五)An octagon shaped toy used as an inside-house decoration for driving out evil spirits.
6. (六) New Year's decorative gift for boys consisting of a bow and arrow (to drive out evil spirits), placed on a long wooden board with a pasted rag picture of a warrior attached to the bottom.
7. (七) A shallow, tub-shaped bucket.
8. (八) Famous place for its autumnal foliage in Nara Prefecture.
9. (九) This drapery was designed for the tast of female servants at samurai mansions.
10. (十) Bamboo sandals with cowhide covering the soles.
11. (十一) Kakekodai a pair of small fishes, tied together with a string through their with ferns attached hung above the enclosed fireplace for cooking inside the house.
12. (十二) A mountain near Kyoto.

Further Analysis

In what kind of society did Saikaku live and work? Seventeenth century Japanese society was based on the Tokugawa (family name) Bakufu (military government) organization. In this organization, hereditary shoguns (highest military leader) controlled all military and administrative power, while the Imperial Court, having relinguished all its power, received, therefore, in return guaranteed incomes and preserved its symbolic leadership status. The main source of income for the authoritarian Tokugawa regime came from the rural population. Farmers were subjected to a tax-rate of 40% or more on their yearly income while the prospering merchant class were almost exempt from taxes in the early Tokugawa Period (1600–1700).

Saikaku was born three years after the newly enforced 'closed country' policy: no Japanese could leave the country; no Catholic foreigner could enter; foreign trade was limited to Protestant Dutch and non-Christian Chinese trading in Nagasaki. Another feature of the early Tokugawa Period was the further development of Japanese ethics called 'bushido'. Obedience was the main ingredient of these ethics, the seeds of which were sown in the fourth century by the Yamato (old name describing Japan poetically and patriotically) chieftains. They had turned their power into a right—and thus obedience into a duty—by having their power endorsed by Kami, the Shinto spirits of their ancestors and the spirits of nature. Early Confucianism was added to this Shinto tradition; sanctifying a strictly hierarchical order. The Tokugawas continued this tradition; enforcing obedience on the whole society (including the emperor). By laws and detailed regulations they created an immobile four-class-society of samurais, farmers, merchants and craftsmen (outcasts, priests ect. were special categories). We can place Saikaku's literary work against the background of the authoritarian Tokugawa regime that ruled over a socially stratified, isolated island nation.

Everlasting Edo Stores can be classified as a distinct product of the author's discourse because it lacks individual character dialogue. Saikaku himself belongs to the well-educated merchants class from which viewpoint he writes, excluding pseudo objective discourse. With 'money' as the central theme, the story's movement enforcements are place and time. Saikaku mentions different places (country, quarters, mountains) in every paragraph, while moving from the middle of December to New Year's Eve and the New Year.

I will deduce a few referential and hypothetical meanings from this story: Referential meanings: 1. Thriving business is done on New Year's Eve. 2. When Kyoto and Osaka people move to Edo, they become more liberal-minded. Hypothetical meanings: 1. Five colored Kyoto drapery suggests a beautiful woman's charm. 2. On New Year's Eve, silver coins whirl and pile up like snow.

Contrasting these meanings with1690 public morals would be difficult and, perhaps unnecessary, because Saikaku's work was read by less than five percent of the population: the members of his class: the well-educated townsmen in Kyoto and Osaka. Still, I can safely assume that in the seventeenth century, the large majority of the Japanese population, the poor, illiterate farmers wouldn't have shared Saikaku's, and his characters', moral values. Nevertheless, Saikaku, himself, built in sharp contrasts regarding reason: the two observations that 'Thriving business is done on New Years Eve' and 'silver coins whirl and pile up like snow' sharply contrast with 'merchants not having the wits to make profit' and 'some people in Edo having less than one gold coin to start New Year'(covering the first referential meaning and the second hypothetical meaning). Saikaku also sharply contrasted Osaka's and Kyoto's people stingy mentality with the liberal-minded disposition of true-bron Edoites. (covering the second referential meaning). That I chose two similes as hypothetical meanings is natural, considering Saikaku's continually using this literary device: 'the footsteps of people sounding like the rumbling of countless carriages,' 'pack-horses transport millions of kilograms of raddishes which looks like fields moving in on foot,' 'money streams in like water,' 'cotton piles...look like snow covering the mountains of Yoshino Town' etc. Saikaku's creation of these stylish and realistic similes gave the story descriptions and ideas of permanent interest.

Finally, I will briefly touch upon the topic of Saikaku's objectivity. In Professor Asao and Professor Fuji's commentary[1] about Saikaku's literary work, they stress many times that Saikaku viewed 'the whirlpool of life' from an 'objective viewpoint'.

First, I have to remark that the highest degree of objectivity can only be achieved by defining and stressing one's own subjectivity. When Saikaku 'refers' to his merchant's experience in the remark, 'it must be mortifying for people who are born as merchants, but not having the wits to make profit,' I consider this as a valuable, subjective contribution to his literary work. In preceding chapters we have observed that writers very often use (consumption-production) material from their own lives and express their own class viewpoint. Regarding Saikaku's work it is obvious when writing 'Peace reigns over our land' and 'money is society's circulating wealth' that he sees the world from a well-educated merchant's viewpoint.

In a closing word about Saikaku, I realize that 'despite' his merchants-viewpoint and the repressive atmosphere in an authoritarian Tokugawa ruled society,

Saikaku had a certain freedom of spirit which he expressed in unique descriptions and stylish, interesting similes.

NOTE

1. Saikaku Ihara, *Sekken Munezanyo,* parallel versions, Isoji Asao and Akio Fuji, Meiji Shoin, Tokyo, 1975.

4

Literary Analysis II

In this chapter I will 'analyse,' to try to understand and explain the 'literary' mechanisms at work in my short story *The Woman In The Red Coat*. Although a short story isn't exactly the same as a novel, I consider the short story as a literary genre that is directly interwoven with the novel; it's a brief prose novel. The sources of inspiration for this story were: 1. the sound of the alarm bells at a railroad crossing near my study in Mishima, 2. a youth memory of Holland, 3. my reading—consumption—of Osamu Dazai's sentence:

> *It seemed the only way was to suddenly grasp, without question, what is simple, natural and clear and put it directly on paper, and this way of thinking allowed me to see the figure of Fuji, in front of me, in a different light.*[1]

I wrote the story in **Japanese** and later made the Dutch and English translations. While working on this story, I will test and verify the practical use—for literary theory—of the following theses and concepts:

1. By exposing unintentional meanings, motives, and understandings that a writer brings into his or her literary work; defining my viewpoint; exposing the writer's viewpoint; framing the writer and his or her literary work in a social-historical context: we can recognize a unified text with a determinate meaning.

2. Multi-language consciousness operates inside the writer and his or her literary work.

3. When using personal experience and thought as the basis of a literary work, a writer can portray an event on the same time-and-value plane as his or her contemporaries.

4. A literary work is in contact with everyday life and the domains of philosophy, religion etc.

5. The concept 'A Cry of the Soul' springs up from a literary work's contents, but to produce this 'Cry of the Soul,' the writer will have to use a method. Could it be Osamu Dazai's method? 'It seemed the only way was to suddenly grasp, without question, what is simple, natural and clear and put it directly on paper, . .'

6. Movement enforcements establish the narrative with its meanings and values.

7. The 'third-person' as created in the character of the rogue, clown, fool etc., corresponds to quasi character's discourse in which the authorial viewpoint is cloaked in the character's discourse.

THE WOMAN IN THE RED COAT

'Kankankan…goo…kankankan' echoed the sound of the alarm bells at the railroad crossing. As I sat in my study, I heard the whizzing sound of the passing train. It reminded me of an incident twenty years before. With a hoe in my hand, I was cutting runners and dead leaves from the strawberry plants in my parents' field. Looking up, by chance, I saw a woman in a bright red coat walking on the path that runs parallel to the railroad line; the railway crossing was a mere two hundred meters away. Naughty boys or lazy people sometimes used this path as a shortcut, but the woman in the red coat was different. (E-1)

Intuitively, inconspicuously, I watched the woman who walked on with a determined step. The moment the woman disappeared from view, my sixth sense made me lay down the hoe and I started walking toward the path. This path ran along the railway that bordered on the back of my parents' fields. In the middle in the back of our fields was a shed from where the path running west along the railway with no overgrowth was clearly visible, but the path that ran east was covered with trees and bushes. Walking slowly, I watched between the trees and under the bushes. After a few minutes my heart suddenly quickened. The flash of the red coat caught my eye. Silently, I sneaked up to within ten meters of the woman to observe her behavior. (E-2)

"Indeed she's waiting for the next train," I thought. Looking at my watch, I noticed that it was twelve minutes before the next train. I hurried to the shed where my father was and asked him to come and help. My mother, who was also in the shed, immediately went home to phone the police. My father's calm attitude and comment surprised me.

'If that woman has the courage, now, to jump in front of the next train, it would be better if we don't interfere.'

'But father,' I retorted, 'we should respect human life. Let's go!'

'I'll go because you asked me to, but some day you might regret this,' my father replied. (E-3)

We stepped over our wire and barbed wire fence and went down the path along the railway to where the woman was sitting. While my father and I stood in front of the woman to block her from jumping, my father started talking to her in a friendly tone,

'Where are you from?'

'... The city of Goes.'

'I know that place very well. During the war I went there regularly by horse and cart to buy oats from a farmer named Jansen. His farm was just in front of the county seat of Zoomdijk, three kilometers from Goes. Do you know Mr. Jansen?'

'....'

'Well, that was thirty years ago, and you aren't that old yet. Today...' my father spoke incessantly. (E-4)

Although I wanted to help the woman, as I stood in front of her with my father, doubts started to form in my mind. The woman's face showed pain and suffering. She was desperate. Her lips quivered slightly. Big drops of perspiration stood out on her forehead.

The railway crossing alarm sounded 'Kankankan,' announcing the coming of the next train. My father and I remained standing in the same place, blocking the woman. The woman's whole body shivered as the train rumbled by at full speed. Watching the woman shiver, I suddenly thought, "My father is right." It seemed like while she was shivering all the strength had drained from her body. (E-5)

'Let's go get a cup of coffee,' my father suggested to the woman.

She answered, 'Yes, thank you.'

The three of us went back to my house. My mother, who was very worried about the woman, tried to cheer her up while making coffee. 'You're beautiful and young...and that red coat looks nice on you.'

What my father had said, that had worked on my conscience so strongly, paled beside my mother's comments trying to cheer the woman up. I thought that surely the way my mother said this woman was beautiful indicated that she would be succesful in society. I wanted so much to believe this. (E-6)

Twenty years ago I didn't know the despair in human life that springs from bitter frustrations and being frustrated. In those days, I thought that everybody could be happy if they went to bars, drank alcohol and played man and woman games.

Drinking coffee, the cup shook in the woman's trembling hands. Although I had been the one who found the woman on my own initiative and had kept her from committing suicide, sitting across from her I didn't say a word. "Is my mother right, or is my father right?" This question swirled through my mind. I tried to read the answer from the *woman's facial expression, her beautiful blue eyes clearly expressing her mental suffering. As I reflected on these confused thoughts, the woman started telling us about her life in a psychiatric hospital.* (E-7)

*She had been a patient for two years in the hospital where the doctor tried to suppress her feelings by administering narcotics. Since a week ago, she had pretended that she took the narcotics, ' But secrectely I flushed them down the toilet bowl,' she said. 'That 's why I have just **now** come here with clear judgement.'*

"And then, I had interfered," I realized feeling ashamed.

Avoiding the subject of suicide, my mother continued in her usual way to encourage the woman, 'You aren't wearing a wedding ring. Are you still single?' my mother asked.

'Yes,' answered the woman with a quizzical look. (E-8)

'Soon you marry a good husband and your life will change drastically. It's a woman's destiny to care for a husband and children. Surely you'll find a good man in Goes who wants to marry you.'

The expressions 'stress,' 'frustration,' and 'mental suffering' didn't exist in my mother's vocabulary. My mother's love was focused on living for the good of the family and sacrificing herself for the family. The woman who had been contemplating suicide may have thought my mother's comments were critical. The woman lived alone and didn't care for a husband or children. She had lived a rather self-centered existence.

'Tontonton' sounded a tapping on the door. My mother went to answer the door and, in a short time returned. (E-9)

'Eh…two friendly policemen are waiting outside…They will take you back to the hospital by car,' my mother said with some embarrassment in her voice. The woman stood up mechanically.

'Thank you for the coffee. Yes, it's time to go back,' she said as she left the kitchen. My father and I followed her to the door.

'We're sorry to be late, but we're very busy,' one of the policeman said to my father. The other policeman spoke to the woman with a smile, 'It's just as well that you didn't jump in front of the train. The cleaning up afterwards is always horrible…arms and legs scattered here and there. The last time I couldn't find the fellow's set of teeth.'

The woman got startled into the police car. (E-10)

It was a sunny autumn day.

The sunshine reflected on the white police car as it drove out of sight.

The policeman's crude comments had disturbed me.

The wind got stronger and intensified the sound that pervaded my consciousness, 'kankankankankan...' (E-11)

An Analysis Of The Story *The Woman in The Red Coat.*

While I contemplated the contents, technique and style to be used for writing a new novel, I read Osamu Dazai's sentence: 'It seemed the only way was to suddenly grasp, without question, what is simple, natural and clear and put it directly on paper, and this way of thinking allowed me to see the figure of Fuji, in front of me, in a different light.'

While reading this passage, the alarm bells at the railroad crossing near my study sounded and I remebered, in the first place, the alarm bells of the railroad crossing near my parents' home. The similar sounds of the alarm bells—the same in Holland as in Japan—but with a gap of twenty years in my real life time, made me wonder about the meaning of life. I had travelled halfway around the world to live again near a railroad. What a coincidence. I'm not a railroad enthusiast but somehow railroads seem to cross my life path. I started to compare my different experiences of life near a railroad in Holland and Japan. One striking difference I remembered immediately. Although the suicide rate in Japan is probably higher than in Holland, the railroad near my parents' home was often used by patients from a psychiatric hospital, to commit suicide. The railroad behind my study in Mishima is never used for that purpose.

Reminiscing about railroads, suicides and my late father's advice; 'Son, never go and look at the scenes of those committed suicides on the railroad. You won't be able to sleep or eat for a couple of days,' I remembered one incident when my father and I prevented a suicide. This memory, I wanted to write down in a short story based on Osamu Dazai's methodology! I started 'Kankankan...goo...kankankan' which would have been a strange, impossible beginning in standard Dutch language because we don't express the innumerable 'natural' sounds that exist in the Japanese vocabulary of onomatopoeic words. It's because of Osamu Dazai's methodology that I brougth new words into the Dutch and English languages (thesis 2) and that I used the 'sound' as the movement enforcement of this short story. (Suddenly grasp, without question, what is simple, natural and clear,...)

At the time of the incident, I was a student, perhaps twenty years old, in Holland; at the time of writing the story I was about forty years old. The gap of twenty years between the incident and writing about it, gave me time to fantasize: in passage 1, did I really look by chance or was I just idling, waiting for the coffee break or lighting up a cigarette? The choice of 'by chance' seemed to me to arouse the readers' curiosity; by chance and then, what happened?

Moreover, the choice of 'the red coat' is probably a falsification of truth; an unintentional falsification! I only remembered that the woman wore bright clothes and perhaps she didn't wear a coat but a two-piece suit. Let's assume it would have been, in reality, a yellow and green, polka dot two-piece suit:—closer to reality—words describing this wouldhaveresultedintheunattractivestorytitleof: **THE WOMAN IN THE YELLOW AND GREEN POLKA-DOT, TWO-PIECE SUIT'** This detailed title might suit a fashion catalog but it would be too long for the title of a literary work; it diverts the readers' attention from the focus on **that** woman.

In summary (about the opening passage), my multi-languaged consciousness made the openings sentence possible for the English and Dutch versions. The gap of twenty years between experiencing the incident and the writing of the story, created time for an unintentional falsification that I combined with my present literary knowledge: a title has to be short, attractive, appetizing, and invite the reader to start reading etc. And Osamu Dazai's sentence inspired me to use the movement enforcement of sound and silence (thesis 1).

The second passage is a truthful description of my feelings and actions—as far as I can remember—at the time of the incident. The chronotope of space works in this passage: fields, shed, path, bushes and trees. I had to **walk slowly** to have a good look between the trees and under the bushes. Are 'intuitively' and 'the sixth sense' mini-cries from the story's contents or from the writer's soul? We will have to keep this question open.

The third passage's 'twelve minutes' is an almost perfect deduction and my father's comment is true memory. That time, his comment stunned me and with the passing of twenty years, it still confuses me, but I started to understand that it can be cruel to prevent someone from committing suicide in certain situations. As a writer, I grasped my father's reply and my surprise from twenty years ago. I didn't bring any unintentional meaning, motive and understanding into this passage. I grasped, without question, that what is simple and natural; especially my father's prophesy, '*someday you might regret this.*' (thesis 1)

This prophesy exemplifies the meaning of portraying an event on the same time-and-value plane as my contemporaries, because '**some day**' indicates that at the present of the incident I differed in opinion from my father, but my opinion may change in the future. Different opinions can be based on a shared—in common—value plane; therefore my suprise (thesis 3).

I fantasized my father's speech in the fourth passage, although I remember that my father continued talking to the woman. Probably he wanted to divert her attention from committing suicide, but while writing the story, I didn't remember the contents of my father's talk. That's why I used one of my father's stories from the war. While my father was talking, I was more occupied with the coming of the next train and I was inwardly cursing the expected late arrival of the police. In this fourth passage, my father's incessantly speaking—sound—is meant to divert the woman's attention from suicide; but what's the meaning and value of the woman's silence? It can mean agreement or disagreement with my father's talk; or she might not have listened to his words: being involved in an inner-struggle: a struggle of the soul without a cry. The meaning of silence is open to endless speculation (thesis 5).

After the woman's silence, my father talks on, which gives me (as the character in the story) time to observe the woman until the alarm bells at the railroad crossing sound again 'Kankankankan,' (in the fifth passage). This sound causes four actions: 1. father and I blocking the woman, 2. the train rumbling by, 3. the woman's shivering and 4. my thinking. Unintentionally, according to the way this accident really occured, I realize now that the woman's previous silence—struggle of the soul without a cry—is being connected and reinforced by the woman's shivering. She didn't burst out shrieking, no instead the woman's silence is in a natural way tied up with her shivering. This silence of her soul, of her body—no shrieking—, forms a beautiful contrast with the sound of the alarm bells and the rumbling train. And her silent inner-struggle finds (by way of shivering) its expression in my silent thought, "Father is right." Without a pre-fabricated plot etc., I was able to grasp, without question, what is simple, natural and clear; I could extract the kernel of that incident-situation where the woman was sitting and my father and I blocking her way (thesis 5).

Coming to passages six and seven, I realize that my part in the story was closer to being an observer than an active participant. I speak only one sentence in the complete story: 'But father,' I retorted,' we should respect human life. Let's go.' I recreated myself as the observing third-person (thesis 7) in the story; listening to and weighing my father's and mother's opinions and trying to understand the woman's behavior. Who was right, my father or mother? This question expresses an idea of permanent and universal interest. At a sudden moment, when there is no time to study the medical record, background etc., of an unknown person who is at the point of committing suicide; do we have to prevent this person's suicide or leave it up to that person's will? This question brings my story in contact with everyday life, the domains of religion, moral values etc. (thesis 4).

The woman's '**now**' in passage 8; 'That's why I have just, **now** come here with clear judgement,' is directly linked up with my father's '**now**' in passage 3: 'If that woman has the courage, **now**, to jump in front of the next train, it would be better if we don't interfere.' In this case, the movement enforcement of time is at work.

The movement enforcement of time—now—, the extracting of the kernel in passage 5, my position as the third-person, etc., requires a deeper analysis to lay bare the mechanisms that are at work inside this story. That's why I return to passage 5 and will define the movement enforcements, the various—referential, hypothetical and regular—meanings and their moral values. A relationship might exist between the movement enforcements, meanings and values.

The movement enforcement is the sound 'kankankan' that caused the four actions: 1. father and I blocking the woman, 2. the train rumbling by, 3. the woman's shivering and 4. my thought (thesis 6). 'The place' beside the railroad isn't described at all. This isn't necessary for the plot and it wouldn't have produced a better story if I had written: The train rumbled by at full speed at a distance of less than one meter from the pebbled walk where father and I were standing. 'Unintentionally' I had chosen the movement enforcement of sound and the woman's silence; I didn't want to add too much diverting information (thesis 1).

Passage 5 gives the following meanings;

Referential meanings: 1. I was wavering about my decision to prevent the woman from committing suicide. 2. The woman—in a deep inner-struggle—lacked the determination to jump.

Hypothetical meanings; 1. The woman was in pain and suffering; she was desperate. 2. My father was right (to let her jump in front of the train). 3. The woman's shivering had drained all the strength from her body.

Regular meaning: My father and I prevented a desperate woman from committing suicide.

The sound movement enforcement stopped my wavering about my decision (referential meaning 1) and it brought to an end the first hypothetical meaning and it produced the second and third hypothetical meanings. The central role of movement enforcement elements (time, space, sound etc.); their creating role of narrative and meanings is to be considered as a pivotal mechanism of literary production.

Now I will place the referential and hypothetical meanings in my previously used moralistic classification schedule (part I of this dissertation). I consider the 'I' narrator, i.e., myself as the story's discourse carrier!

story title	meanings	no	discourse carrier moral	Public moral
The Woman in the Red Coat **passage 5**	Referential meanings	(1)	true good	true bad
		(2)	true bad/good	true good
	Hypothetical meanings	(1)	true bad	true bad
		(2)	untrue bad true good	untrue bad
		(3)	untrue bad	true good

Except for the first hypothetical meaning, all the other meanings contain contrasts between the story's character's and the public moral. It's noteworthy that the movement enforcement of sound creates contrast between the discourse carrier's and the public moral for the second and third hypothetical meanings.

To build up a theory, we have to compare our result from passage five with the analyses of more passages. The passages ten and eleven are started by the knocking sound in passage nine and close by the sound of alarm bells at the railroad. Passages nine and ten give the following meanings; Referential meanings: 1. The woman had regained control over her inner-struggle. 2. The policeman's comments revived the woman's inner-struggle. 3. The sound that pervaded my consciousness was the sound at the time of the incident or the sound at the time I was writing the story.

Hypothetical meanings: 1. My mother was embarrased to introduce the policemen. 2. The policeman crude comments had disturbed me.

Classification according to moral:

story title	meanings	no	discourse carrier moral	Public moral
The Woman in the Red Coat **passage 9-10**	Referential meanings	(1)	untrue bad	true good
		(2)	true bad	true bad
		(3)	× ×	× ×
	Hypothetical meanings	(1)	true bad	true good
		(2)	true bad	true good

The third referential meaning, which is basically the sound 'kankankan,' doesn't fit into the moralistic classification schedule. The same can be said about the knocking sound on the door. Of course, sounds and silence do have meanings; but it's impossible to judge their moral value.

In conclusion: the regular use of movement enforcements in combination with the creation of hypothetical meanings that contain sharp moral contrasts between the story character's and the public moral, are essential ingredients of literature. The seven theses stated at the beginning of this chapter, can be added to the previously found mechanisms (Part I of this dissertation) that are at work in literature and literary production.

1. The writer processes his or her thoughts, feelings, impressions, echoes that emanate from his or her life in a functioning society, into a literary product.

2. The writer's main tool 'language knowledge' has been largely set and predetermined.

3. Language functions have a consumptive as well as a productive nature, which may interrelate, influence and run over into each other.

4. Language functions form a unity in variety that through the writer are fused into an organic literary product.

5. Literary production is subjected to the market mechanisms of present capitalistic society; it has to turn out a profit.

6. A literary product can't be something completely new or unique, although processed through the writer in a unique form or style, expressing ideas of permanent or universal interest, it may provide artistic joy to mankind for centuries.

7. A writer brings unintentional meanings, motives and understandings into his or her literary work.

8. From different viewpoints—psychological, social-political, historical etc.—we can establish different interpretations of a literary work.

9. While a writer uses various techniques—choice of discourse and speech type—bases his or her writing on different production processes: it's the contrast between the discourse carrier and the public moral values for the various meanings that has to be the essenttial ingredient of his or her literature.

10. Class-struggle influences language.

11. Language (ideological language) influences class struggle.

12. Incorrectly signifying meaning is the source of the disunity between material-social activity and language.

13. By exposing unintentional meanings, motives and understandings that a writer brings into his or her literary work; defining my viewpoint; exposing the writer's viewpoint; framing the writer and his or her literary work in a social-historical context, I can recognize a unified text with a determinate meaning.

14. Multi-language consciousness operates inside the writer and his or her literary work.

15. When using personal experience and thought as the basis of a literary work, a writer can portray an event on the same time-and-value plane as his or her contemporaries.

16. A literary work is in contact with every day life and the domains of philosophy, religion etc.

17. The concept of 'A Cry Of The Soul' springs up from a literary's work's contents, but to produce this 'cry' we will have to use Osamu Dazai's method: 'It seemed the only way was to suddenly grasp, without question what is simple, natural and clear and put it directly on paper…'

18. Movement enforcements establish the narrative with its meanings and values.

19. The 'third person' as created in the character of the rogue, clown, fool or recreated by the writer in the 'I' character of himself or herself inside the story corresponds to a quasi character's discourse in which the authorial viewpoint is cloaked in the character's discourse.

NOTE

1. Osamu Dazai, *Ogon Fukei*, Tokyo, Shinchosha, 18th edition, 1998, translated by L. G. Perkins.

PART 3

A MARXIST APPROACH TO JAPANESE LITERATURE

1

K. Marx, F. Engels, V. I. Lenin and L. Trotsky

Despite Karl Marx's disagreement about using Marxism as the name for his 'world view', it has become the generally accepted term for his and Engels' economical and political theory. Ernest Mandel[a] gave the following description of Marxism: 'In the last analysis, Marxism is the product of the appearance of the capitalist mode of production in certain regions of Western Europe..., beginning in the fifteenth and sixteenth centuries and leading to the emergence of a new bourgeois society that gradually came to dominate all spheres of human activity.'[1]

This description leaves no doubt about Marx and Engels being the products of their time; of capitalist society. Marx and Engels analysed, explained and predicted the tendencies of the fundamental mechanisms of the capitalist mode of production. However, they weren't the revolutionary prophets that made blueprints for revolutions as they are often wrongly described and or supposed to have done.

Marx and Engels' views on literature. In a letter [2] to Ferdinand Lassalle[b], Marx applauds both composition and action of Lassale's play 'Franz von Sickinger'. Another important value that Marx attaches to the play is its inducement of the reader's excitement. Having noted these positive values, Marx observes that Lassalle might, 'have put a touch more artistry into the iambics—since you have chosen to write in verse.'

At the same time, Marx attaches to this lack of artistry a positive merit because it shocks the professional poets. Furthermore, Marx points out that the character of Sickingen can be compared to the cultivated aristocracy of 1830, who, 'turned themselves on the one hand into the organs of modern ideas while on the other actually representing a reactionary class interest.' Because of chosing this character—Sickingen—Lassalle's story gets the main idea of civic unity, whereas, according to Marx the significant and dynamic background of the story should have been based on the representatives of the peasants and the revolutionary elements in the town. 'Then you would automatically have had to 'Shakespearise' more, whereas your principal failing is, to my mind 'Shillering' [c], i.e. using individuals as mere mouthpieces for the spirit of the times.' In this letter, Marx's approach to literature is very traditional—composition, technique, excitement—and the act of correctly describing the class struggle he turns into 'Shakespearising'.

In the same period of time, spring 1859, Engels wrote his opinion[3] about the same play to Lassalle. Engels appreciates Lassalle's 'skilful manipulation of the plot and the thoroughly dramatic nature of the piece.' Engels also remarks: 'it seems to me that a person is not characterised merely by what he does, but also how he does it; and in this respect it would, I think, have done the intellectual content of the play no harm had clearer distinctions and stronger contrast been drawn between individual characters.' Engels refers here to the importance of Shakespeare.

Having discussed the formal aspects of the play, Engels turns next to the historical content. Similar to Marx, he observes that Lassalle, 'had failed to lay due emphasis [upon] the non-official, plebeian and peasant elements, with their concomitant theoretical representation.' Engels writes that if Lassalle had provided the material of 'vagabond beggar kings, hungry mercenaries and adventerures of all kinds' then their portrayal could have been 'more effective than in Shakespeare.'

In the latter part of his letter Engels writes more about the political short-comings of Lassalle's play by which 'the truly tragic element in Sickingen's fate' escaped to Lassalle. From these two letters of Marx and Engels, we learn that both of them use traditional literary concepts of plot (manipulation, technique), description of characters (contrasting, 'Shakespearising') and refer to Shakespeare as a standard for comparison. They attach great importance to the correct portrayal and use of the class struggle.

---

[a] Ernest Mandel (1923–1995), widely acknowledged as the foremost Marxist economist, editor, occupied leading positions in the Socialist Workers Party and the Fourth International.

[b] Ferdinand Lassalle (1825–1864), founder of the first German Workers Party.

In summary, from a Marxist viewpoint a text shoud have to be read in relation to the theory of historical materialism which, 'designates that view of history which seeks the ultimate cause and the great moving power of all important historic events in the economic development of society, in the changes of modes of production and exchange, in the consequent division of society into distinct classes, and in the struggle of these classes against one another.' [4]

V. I. Lenin. Lenin was undoubtedly an influential political leader and theorist of 'Marxism' in the twentieth century. Between the Russian Revolutions of 1905 and 1917, Lenin wrote a few articles about the Russian writer Leo Tolstoy (1828–1910). According to Lenin, Tolstoy and his work are the embodiment of the first Russian Revolution. The same weakness and strength that Lenin finds in this revolution, are also to be found in Tolstoy's works.

Lenin sees Tolstoy's work as the peasants' protest against tyranny and serfdom. However, Tolstoy's renunciation of politics, his doctrine of 'non-resistance to evil' led Tolstoy away from involvement with the Russian proletarian struggle for emancipation.

Lenin states that Tolstoy's attitude toward the struggle was apathetic; his works, which belong to the past, contain criticisms of church, state and capitalism that will instill a consciousness in the masses. The masses will have to learn the meanings of these criticisms to destroy the tsarist monarchy and landlordism. In this way Tolstoy's literature contributes to the revolution. In the article *Leo Tolstoy and His Epoch*, Lenin quotes the following passage from Tolstoy's book *Anna Karenina:*

> *"Talk about the harvest, hiring labourers, and so forth, which, as Levin knew, it was the custom to regard as something very low,...now seemed to Levin to be the only important thing. 'This, perhaps, was unimportant under serfdom, or is unimportant in England. In both cases the conditions are definite; but here today, when everything has been turned upside down and is only just taking shape again, the question of how these conditions will shape is the only important question in Russia,' mused Levin."* (Collected Works, Vol. X, p. 137.) [5]

Lenin remarks that Tolstoy observes the disappearance of serfdom and conceives the new bourgeois order only vaguely, 'in the form of a bogey-England.' Tolstoy didn't want to investigate—consider the extremely varied forms that the bourgeois system had assumed in England.

---

^c Friedrich von Shiller (1759–1805), German poet, dramatist, and philosopher.

Lenin states furthermore: 'He [Tolstoy] reasons in the abstract, he recognizes only the standpoint of the eternal principles of morality, the eternal truths of religion, failing to realise that this standpoint is merely the ideological reflection of the old ("turned upside down") order, the feudal order, the way of the life of the Oriental peoples.' [6]

Lenin ascibed to Tolstoy an ideology that fitted with the period of upheaval in Russia from 1862–1905. An ideology of asceticism, 'non-resistance to evil', a faith in the Spirit etc., that corresponds to the people's ingrained beliefs, habits and traditions. During this period of upheaval, [the masses] 'do not and cannot see what kind of new order is taking shape, what social forces are shaping it and how, what social forces are capable of bringing release from the incalculable and exceptionally acute distress that is characteristic of epochs of upheaval,' [7] Lenin describes Tolstoy's ideology as 'utopian' and 'reactionary', but he also sees 'socialistic' and 'critical elements' in it that 'are capable of providing valuable material for the enlightment of the advanced classes.' [8]

Lenin, like Marx and Engels, approaches literature in relation to the theory of historical materialism. I want to stress, though, that Lenin's general concept of literature (and art) isn't Marxist in the literal sense of this world view. Marx's understanding of economics, philosophy, art etc., was at an unattainable level for Lenin. This is the proper place to quote Engels: 'What Marx accomplished I would not have achieved. Marx stood higher, saw further, and took a wider and quicker view than all the rest of us. Marx was a genius; we others were at best talented.' [9]

When Marx speaks about art and literature, he stresses artistic 'taste', 'beauty' and 'aesthetic pleasure.' [10] Marx doesn't use Leninistic labels such as 'reactionary' or 'socialistic' for mainstream literature and writers such as Homer, M. de Cervantes Saaveda and Balzac. Lenin's viewpoint that socialism would be a long revolutionary process between a capitalist and communist society is another angle from which to condemn Lenin's theories because this process hadn't started in Rusia of 1910 nor in Russia of 1917. In a reversed way of reasoning, we can say that Tolstoy's 'utopian and reactionary ideology' was very revolutionary because of his sharp criticisms. Tolstoy could develop these criticisms, just because 'he reasons in the abstract, he recognises only the standpoint of "eternal" principles'; these are Lenin's words used in a reversed way. Lenin's statement that Tolstoy should have had to investigate the bourgeois system of England is too absurd to be taken seriously: an artist can be, but in general isn't, a social scientist. It would have been utterly nonsense to have demanded from Vincent van Gogh to investigate the social and political conditions in Holland at the time when he was painting a poor Dutch family eating their meager meal of potatoes.

Lenin's mechanical-forced connection between Tolstoy's works and the period of upheaval in Russia is rejectable from a Marxist viewpoint. Marx states very clearly: 'As regard art, it is known that certain periods of its florescence by no means correspond to the general development of society, or, therefore, to the material basis, the skeleton as it were of its organisation. For example the Greeks compared to the moderns, or else Shakespeare.' [11]

To bring art and literature in relation to the theory of historical materialism isn't sufficient. Marx writes: 'The difficulty is that they [Greek art and poetry] still give us aesthetic pleasure and are in certain respects regarded as a standard and unattainable model.' [12] Marx gives the following explanation about understanding and appreciating art:

> *An adult cannot become a child again, or he becomes childish. But does not the naiveté of the child give him pleasure, and must he not himself endeavour to reproduce the child's veracity on a higher level? Does not the specific character of every epoch come to live again in its natural veracity in the child's nature? Why should not the historical childhood of humanity, where it attained its most beautiful form, exert an eternal charm as a stage that will never recur?...The charm their [the Greeks'] art has for us does not conflict with the immature stage of the society in which it originated. On the contrary, that charm is a consequence of this and is, rather, inseperably linked with the fact that the immature social conditions which gave rise, and which alone could give rise, to this art can never recur.* [13]

Marx's view is dialectical; the interconnection of processes advancing by leaps and bounds; the dialectics of history based on real and concrete human beings; 'the real emancipation movement progressively unfolding throughout history, with its leaps forwards and grave setbacks.'[14] Marx's view is very human and pure: 'Reproduce the child's veracity on a higher level' and respectful towards art that can find its roots in a society which is still in an immature stage.

Leon Trotsky. Trotsky (1879–1940), was the leader of the Russian Revolutions in 1905 and 1917; and People's Commissar for Foreign Affairs and for Military and Naval Affairs from 1918 to 1925. From 1923 Trotsky led opposition movements in the Politburo against the Soviet Bureaucracy. In 1927, he was expelled from the party and in 1929 Stalin expelled him from Russia. Trotsky

formed the Fourth International (1938) to oppose Stalinism and he was assassi-
nated by a Stalin's agent in Mexico in 1940.

In the summers of 1922–23, Trotsky wrote the article *Literature and Revolution*. The article's opening paragraph stresses the importance of solving the economic problems because if these aren't solved the proletarian regime will cease to
exist. We need to remark that Trotsky never considered the Soviet Union as a
socialist society; merely a society that is stationed between capitalism and socialism; a society that might progress towards socialism or regress into capitalism.
Trotsky considers the old Russian literature as the expression of the nobleman
and the bureaucrat and which is based on the peasant. He observes, from the
beginning of the twentieth century up to the beginning of the First World War
(1914), the powerful uprising of the petty bourgeois intellectuals and their literature, which ended because of the war. After the Russian revolution (1917), literature that's built up around the bourgeoisie's life doesn't exist any longer. Instead,
the writer must choose between the peasant and the proletarian. This choice is
difficult for the intellectual because he doesn't belong to either class. According to
Trotsky, bourgeoisie society created a contradition between intellectual work,
including art, and physical work. In spite of being the leader of the revolution the
proletarian only undertakes physical labor. Trotsky states that one of the ultimate
aims of the Revolution is to overcome the seperation between physical labor [car-
ried out by the leaders of the Revolution], and intellectual work [performed by
the former bourgeoisie].

Having seen some of Trotky's ideas, it's necessary to make a few critical comments. Trotsky and Lenin, two intellectuals who never did any physical labor,
were the leaders of the Bolshevik Party that after having captured a majority in
the principal urban and military Soviets, seized power in a coup. The proletarians
may have supported the revolution but they were never the leaders. This can be
explained from the fact that the Bolshevik Party first used the Soviets to stir up
the revolution and to seize power and consequently transformed the Soviets into
subordinate organs of the dictatorial state bureaucracy. Instead of Marx's and
Engels' envisioned society: 'an association, in which the free development of each
is the condition for the free development of all,'[15] Lenin and Trotsky laid the
foundations of a dictatorial state bureaucracy in which the workers and the peasants were exploited, surpressed, deported and executed.

Trotsky gives a deformed interpretation: although he is the intellectual leader
of the revolution, he states that the proletariat is the leader. He denies his own
leading and intellectual contribution to the revolution. Besides, Trotsky's explanation is contradictory; if the proletariat only undertakes physical labor, then it

would be impossible for them to be the leader of such a gigantic, **intellectually** planned undertaking like the Russian Revolution.

In reference to revolutionary art and socialist art Trotsky states: 'It is fundamentally incorrect to contrast bourgeois culture and bourgeois art with proletarian culture and proletarian art. The latter will never exist, because the proletarian régime is temporary and transient.'[16] About socialist art of the future Trotsky writes:

> *One cannot tell whether revolutionary art will succeed in producing "high" revolutionary tragedy. But socialist art will revive tragedy. Without God, of course. The new art will be atheist. It will also revive commedy, because the new man of the future will want to laugh. It will give new life to the novel. It will grant all rights to lyrics, because the new man will love in a better and stronger way than did the old people, and he will think about the problems of birth and death. The new art will revive all the old forms which arose in the course of the development of the creative spirit. The disintegration and decline of these forms are not absolute, that is, they do not mean that these forms are are absolutely incompatible with the spirit of the new age. All that is necessary is for the poet of the new epoch to re-think in a new way the thoughts of mankind, and to re-feel its feeling...* [17]

Trotsky's observations about art don't bring us nearer to a better understanding of literature and literary production. He doesn't analyse any literary work, neither does he consider forms of art such as painting, sculpture and music. Trotsky's general remarks about art and culture convey solely his political ideas. For example, the statement that 'proletarian art will never exist' is obviously correct from Trotsky's political viewpoint that the proletarian only undertakes physical labor! However, it is wrong to base this statement upon the observation that 'the proletarian régime is temporary and transient'. Not only is 'the proletarian régime' temporary: Marxism's dialectical view means that all reality is a whole in motion and in continual change, with leaps forwards and grave setbacks. Trotsky's 'proletarian régime' is a part of this reality! Trotsky's gives a static quality to his 'temporary régime' that is opposed to Marxist dialectics which 'regards every historically developed form as being in a fluid state, in motion. .' [18] Ascribing a 'static' quality to a 'temporary régime' sounds like double Dutch but it's the outcome of Trotsky's reasoning that proletarian art will never exist. Disregarding the labeling of 'bourgeois' and 'socialist' art, which doesn't make any sense—were Vincent van Gogh's paintings bourgeois art?

Art is created in a society that is based on the capitalist mode of production: art can also be created in a society that is based on the socialist mode of production as well as in a society that is based on a temporary mode of production under a proletarian régime.

Trotsky's notion that 'socialist art' will revive the tragedy, comedy and the novel, isn't compatible with Marx's and Engels' theory of history. Marx states that certain artistic forms like Greek epic are only possible, can only reach their level as a 'standard and unattainable model' in an undeveloped society. The undeveloped state of the Greek society was a condition to create art based upon the harmony between Man and Nature. This harmony is destroyed by the bourgeoisie and its capitalist mode of production; with its ever developing division of labor: [the bourgeoisie] 'has resolved personal worth into exchange value…The bourgeoisie has stripped of its halo every occupation hitherto honoured and looked up to with reverent awe. It has converted the physician, the lawyer, the priest, the poet, the man of science, into its paid wage-labourers.'[19]

Marx and Engels don't pity the destruction of the harmony between Man and Nature: it's part of society's progress.

> When the ancient world was in its last throes, the ancient religions were overcome by Christianity. When Christean ideas succumbed in the 18th century to rationalist ideas, feudal society fought its death battle with the revolutionary bourgeoisie. [20]

It's the concept of progress—revolutionary movement—that underlies Marx's and Engels' concept of history, also in regard to the bourgeoisie:

> Bourgeois society is the most developed and many-faceted historical organization of production. [21]

Marx and Engels combine this concept of progress with the necessary alteration of men.

> Both for the production on a mass scale of this communist consciousness, and for the succes of the cause itself, the alteration of men on a mass scale is necessary, an alteration which can only take place in a practical movement, a revolution; the revolution is necessary therefore, not only because the ruling class cannot be overthrown in any other way, but also because the class overthrowing it can only in a revolution succeed in ridding itself of all the muck of ages and become fitted to found a new society anew. [22]

Men in possession of a communist consciousness ridding themselves 'of all the muck of ages', certain artistic forms linked up with the degree of undevelopment—development—of a society; these Marxist concepts don't leave any room for Trotsky's concept of reviving bygone artistic forms. Moreover, Trotsky's poet (artist) will not exist in the socialist future; at least according to Marx and Engels:

> *in communist society, where nobody has one exclusive sphere of activity but each can become accomplished in any branch he wishes, society regulates in general production and this makes it possible for me to do one thing today and another tomorrow, to hunt in the morning, fish in the afternoon, rear cattle in the evening, criticise after dinner, just as I have a mind, without ever becoming hunter, fisherman, shepherd or critic.* [23]

Concludingly, we have observed that, between, on the one hand Marx and Engels and on the ohter Lenin and Trotsky, enormous discrepancies exist in their respective views on art and literature. Lenin's **mechanical**—forced—connection between literature and a certain epoch doesn't agree with Marxism: Trotsky's political views that proletarian art will never exist, the lack of Marxism's dialectics and Trotsky's reviving of old, bygone, artistic forms is contradictory to Marxism's concept of progress.

Despite these discrepancies, lack and contradictions; leading 'Marxist' critics such as Terry Eagleton[c] and Pierre Macherey[d] unjustly treat, Lenin's and Trotsky's theories as an integral part of Marxism. P. Macherey describes Lenin's contributions on Tolstoy as 'exceptional work in the history of scientific Marxism.' [24] T. Eagleton dwells upon Lenin and Trotsky as orthodox Marxist critics in his book 'Marxism and Literary Criticism.'[25]

To avoid misunderstandings I think that it's necessary to limit the use of 'Marxist'—'Marxism' only to Marx's and Engels' theories! Marxism's deviants such as Leninism, Stalinism and Trotskyism and their originators ought to be kept separate from the human and critical Marxism which was developed by Marx and Engels.

---

[c] Terry Eagleton (1943–) is Tutorial Fellow at Wadham College and Lecturer in English at Oxford University.

[d] Pierre Macherey, Marxist philosopher, who works from within the French Communist Party.

NOTES

1. Ernest Mandel, *The Place of Marxism in History*, New Jersey, Humanities Press, 1994, p. 1.

2. Karl Marx/ Frederick Engels, Collected Works 40, New York, International Publishers, Copyright Progress Publishers, Moscow, 1983, p. 419.

3. Ibid., pp. 441-446.

4. A Dictionary of Marxist Thought, edited by T. Bottomore, UK, Oxford, Blackwell Publishers, Second Revised Edition 1991, p. 234.

5. V. I. Lenin, *On Art and Literature*, Collected Works Vol. 17, Moscow, Progress Publishers, 1968, p. 49.

6. Ibid., p. 50.

7. Ibid., p. 51.

8. Ibid., p. 52.

9. F. Engels, *Ludwig Feuerbach and the outcome of Classical German Philosophy*, New York, International Publishers, ninth printing, 1988, p. 43.

10. Karl Marx/ Frederick Engels, Collected Works Vol. 28, New York, International Publishers, Copyright Progress Publishers Moscow, 1986, pp. 30 and 47.

11. Ibid., p. 46.

12. Ibid., p. 47.

13. Ibid., pp. 47-48.

14. Ernest Mandel, *The Place of Marxism in History*, New Jersey, Humanities Press, Copyright Ernest Mandel 1986, p. 17.

15. Karl Marx/ Frederick Engels, *Manifesto of the Communist Party*, Second Revised edition, Moscow, Progress Publishers, 1977, p. 60.

16. L. Trotsky, *The Age of Permanent Revolution*, A Trotsky Anthology, New York, Dell, 1964, p. 319.

17. Ibid., pp. 319-320.

18. Karl Marx, *Capital,* Vol. 1, London, Penguin Classics, 1990, p. 103.

19. Karl Marx/ Frederick Engels, *Manifesto of the Communist Party*, Second Revised edition, Moscow, Progress Publishers, 1977, p. 38.

20. Ibid., p. 57.

21. Karl Marx/ Frederick Engels, Collected Works Vol. 28, New York, International Publishers, Copyright Progress Publishers Moscow, 1986, p. 42.

22. Karl Marx/ Frederick Engels, *The German Ideology*, Collected Works, Vol. 5, Moscow, Progress Publishers1976, p. 53.

23. Ibid., p. 47.

24. Pierre Macherey, *A Theory of Literary Production*, English Translation, London, Routledge&Kegan Paul, 1978, p. 105.

25. T. Eagleton, *Marxism and Literary Criticism*, University of California Press, Berkeley and Los Angeles, 1976.

2

A Marxist Literary Theory

Marx's and Engels' aesthetic views are based mainly on their ideas about literature, but their dispersed comments in correspondence and political and economical writings don't form a comprehensive literary theory. Although 'Marxist' critics have developed literary theories; their concepts are generally based on faulty interpretations of Marxism. We observed that Lenin and Trotsky are described wrongly as Marxist critics: in this chapter, I will develop Marxist theses for literary theory while briefly considering some of those faulty interpretations.

I formulated in Part I the first Marxist thesis about language: class struggle influences language. I stated that the most current meanings of words—language—conform to the ideas of the ruling class of that epoch and might be determined by that ruling class. Once more I will take the quotation—but in expanded form—from which I deduced that Marxist thesis.

> *The ideas of the ruling class are in every epoch the ruling ideas: i.e., the class which is the ruling material force of society is at the same time its ruling intellectual force. The class which has the means of material production at its disposal, consequently also controls the means of mental production, so that the ideas of those who lack the means of mental production are on the whole subject to it.* [1]

We need to supplement this quotation from Marx's and Engels' work *The German Ideology* with the following information:

> *Remains of the ideologies of old ruling classes can survive long after the end of their rule and exist alongside the current dominant ideology. Ideologies of intermediate classes (such as the petty bourgeoisie in capitalist society), as well as ideologies of newly rising classes, that are revolutionary in relation to the existing ruling classes can also co-exist with it* [the dominant ideology].[2] (E. Mandel)

We can also trace this explicit description by E. Mandel of the co-existence of various ideologies alongside the dominant ideology in Marx's and Engels' writings:

> *When people speak of ideas that revolutionise society, they do but express the fact, that within the old society, the elements of a new one have been created, and that the dissolution of the old ideas keeps even pace with the dissolution of the old conditions of existence.* [3]

> *Bourgeois society is the most developed and many-faceted historical organisation of production. The categories which express its relations, an understanding of its structure, therefore, provide, at the same time, an insight into the structure and the relations of production of all previous forms of society the ruins and components of which were used in the creation of bourgeois society. Some of these remains are still dragged along within bourgeois society unassimilated, while elements which previously were barely indicated have developed and attained their full significance,...* [4]

Marx and Engels adhere to a dialectical view of society's development: outdated components of the structure and the relations of productions that are still dragged along. Their concepts not being limited to economic categories is evident from their explanation about development of religions that follows the foregoing quotation: 'It was not until its self-criticism was to a certain extent prepared, as it were δυναμει, [potentially] that the Christian religion was able to contribute to an objective understanding of earlier mythologies,...' [5]

From the foregoing information, I deduce the following Marxist thesis for literary theory: 1. The author and his or her literary product can be subjected to, can co-exist with, and possibly can revolutionize the dominant ideology.

In the previous chapter, Marx and Engels observed a lack of realistic description in Lassale's play *Franz von Sickinger*. Engels states: 'it seems to me that a person is not characterised merely by what he does, but also how he does it...' Marx notes the lack of 'Shakespearising' in Lassale's play: Lassale elaborated the characters in his play only marginally; he turned his characters into 'mere mouthpieces for the spirit of the times'.

A rich, colorful, realistic description and elaboration of the characters in a play or novel, are essential conditions for Marx and Engels to create acceptable literature. 'Opposed' to these conditions is Marx's and Engels' dislike for a writer's overt partisanship. In a 1885 letter to Minna Kautsky, who had sent him her novel, Engels wrote that: '...the novel primarily finds readers in bourgeois circles,...and there the socialist tendentious novel can fully achieve its purpose, in my view, if, by conscientiously describing the mutual relations, it breaks down the conventionalised illusions dominating them, shatters the optimism of the bourgeois world, causes doubt about the eternal validity of the existing order, and this without directly offering a solution or even, under some circumstances, taking an ostensible partisan stand.' [6]

Marx's statement about the understanding of Greek art: '[the] *endeavour to reproduce the child's veracity on a higher level,'* is in combination with Marx's and Engels' stress on a conscientious and realistic description of relations, illusions, characters etc., without a writer's overt partisanship, the core of the following Marxist thesis for literary theory: 2. Literary production must be based on a writer's unbiased, truthful and 'Shakespearised' description of social reality.

Let's turn our attention, for a moment, to the faulty theories of present-day 'Marxist' critics. E. Balibar and P. Macherey state that an explanation of, 'the specific ideological mode for 'art' and the 'aesthetic' effect...is imposed on Marxism by the dominant ideology...so as to force the Marxist critic to produce his own 'aesthetic'. [7] They propose two alternatives to approach this problem: 'to reject the problem...or to recognise the problem and therefore [to] be forced to acknowledge aesthetic values, i.e.,...to submit to them.' [8] Besides this problem E. Balibar and P. Macherey identify the following problem: 'How to analyse and explain the class position...of the author and more materially the 'literary text' within the ideological class struggle.' [9]

The first problem considers only the dominant ideology without observing the other co-existing ideologies. This disfigured—simplified—ideological reality creates an unreal situation in which the dominant ideology imposes the problem of explaining the specific ideological mode for art and the aesthetic effect on Marxism. There is no ground to prove that the dominant ideology imposes such a trivial problem on Marxism: I can't help seeing it the other way round: two 'Marxist' critics, who don't understand that Marx and Engels turned away from philosophical and ideological criticism[a], imposed this problem on themselves. When discussing art and literature, Marx stresses 'artistic taste', 'beauty' and aesthetic pleasure'. [10] Since beauty is a value and aesthetic pleasure is caused by aesthetic effect, we can conclude that Marx didn't submit himself to 'aesthetic values' but freely acknowledged them!

The second prolem misplaces the author and his or her literary work within the ideological class struggle. Marx and Engels never placed art and literature within the category of ideology. Marx states clearly that art is not determined by the material base of society: 'certain periods of its [art's] florescence by no means correspond to the general development of society.' [11] Also, Marx uses 'eternal charm' when describing the appeal of Greek art: i.e., art has a trans-historical value that, again, can't be determined by the material base of a certain society; therefore art doesn't fit within the category of ideology, which is determined by a society's material base.

How did Marx and Engels explain the writer's class position? There's a unique text from Eleanor Marx (Marx's daughter) about her father's friendship with the German poet Heine[b] in which she writes:

> *It's no exaggeration to say that Morh [Marx's lifelong nickname] not only admired Heine as a poet, but had a sincere affection for him. He would even make all sorts of excuses for Heine's political vagaries. Poets, Mohr maintained, were queer kittle-cattle, not to be judged by the ordinary, or even the extra-ordinary standards of conduct.* [12]

This statement about Heine doesn't relate to a witer's class position, but to his unique human character. Therefore, an analysis and explanation of an author's class position will have to be counterbalanced by considering the writer's unique human nature.

Engels writes about the French novelist Balzac: 'Well, Balzac was politically a Legitimist[c]: his great work is a constant elegy on the irretrievable decay of good society; his sympathies are all with the class doomed to extinction. But for all that, his satyre is never keener, his irony never bitterer than when he sets in motion the very men and women with whom he symphatises most deeply—the nobles.' [13]

Heine was a revolutionary poet for whose 'political vagaries' Marx had to make 'all sorts of excuses'. Balzac is Heine's counterpart in a political spectrum that ranges from revolutionary to conservative views, nevertheless, Engels (Marx likewise in *Capital*) is full of praise for Balzac's literary work. The writer's reactionary, political allegiance is partly disregarded by Marx and Engels. By the same token, Marx and Engels don't judge a literary work according to the 'reactionary' or 'progressive' class values that are incarnated in it; they esteem a transparent description[d] of the characters' ideology[e]. For ultimate clarity I will add this literary yardstick to the second Marxist thesis for literary production: Literary production must be based on a writer's unbiased, truthful and 'Shakespearised' description of social reality including a transparent description of the characters' ideology.

Marx's and Engels' humanistic viewpoint about the writer and his or her class position provides us the core of the third Marxist thesis for literary theory: 3. The writer's class position ought to be counterbalanced by consideration for his or her unique human character.

---

[a] 'The philosophers have **interpreted** the world in various ways: the point however is to change **it**.' [9]

[b] Heinrich Heine (1797–1856), a revolutionary German poet who was exiled to Paris where he met Karl Marx.

[c] Legitimist: a supporter of the elder branch of the Bourbon dynasty to the crown of France.

[d] Various critics define this concept of a transparent description as 'realistic' or 'typicality'. For example S. Morawski writes about Marx's and Engels' aesthetic views: 'Authenticity of realism was to be achieved by, and judged by the expression of a cognitive equivalent: specifically, the dominant and typical traits of socially conflicted life in a particular place and time. Typicality is thus a key consideration.' [14]

[e] Ideology has several meanings in Marxist theories such as a false consciousness, the relationship between inverted consciousness and inverted reality and the general concept used by Engels: the totality of forms of consciousness. I adhere to this 'Engelsistic' concept of ideology.

Classes. If we should analyse and explain the class position of the writer and his or her literary product in relation to the class struggle in capitalist society, we have to understand Marx's and Engels' theory of classes.

In 1848, Marx and Engels write: 'The history of all hitherto existing society is the history of class struggles.'[15] [*Manifesto of the Communist Party*, 1848] Engels adds the following remark in a later edition: That is, all written history. In 1847, the pre-history of society, the social organisation, existing previous to recorded history, was all but unknown…' Engels added this note because in 1884 he had written *The Origin Of The Family, Private Property And The State* for which he had based himself on L. H. Morgan's publication of *Ancient Society* and Marx's notes about this publication. L. H. Morgan was an early American anthropologist who had done extensive research among the North American Indians about their social organisations of family, gens, phratry and tribe. Engels writes in *The Origin:*

> *That is what mankind and human society were like before class divisions arose. And if we compare their condition with that of the overwhelming majority of civilised people today, we will find an enormous gulf between the present-day proletarian and small peasant and the ancient free member of a gens.* [16]

Thus, Marx and Engels were quite aware that class struggles could not be found throughout the whole human history but that they were bound up with certain epochs.

Marx and Engels were also aware of various classes other than bourgeoisie and proletariat in capitalist society. Marx writes in *Theories of Surplus Value*: 'the actual constitution of society, which certainly does not consist merely of the two classes, workers and industrial capitalists,' [17] In *Capital 3*, Marx writes: 'The owners of mere labour-power, the owners of capital and the landowners…in other words wage-labourers, capitalists and landowners—form the three great classes of modern society…Here [England], too, middle and transitional levels always conceal the [class] boundaries…[18] Marx and Engels continually modified their thesis that: 'The history of all hitherto existing society is the history of class struggles.' They observed the non-existence of classes in communal society and similarly as they observed the co-existence of various ideologies alongside the dominant ideology, they described the existence of varous classes alongside bourgeoisie and proletariat.

Furthermore, Marx and Engels fundamentally revised their political theory in response to social-economical developments occuring during their life-time. In 1895, half a year before Engels passed away, he wrote in a new preface to Marx's book *The Class Struggles in France*: 'After the defeats of 1849 we in no way shared the illusions of the vulgar democracy grouped around the would-be provisional governments in partibus.* This vulgar democracy reckoned on a speedy and finally decisive victory of the "people" over the "usurpers"; we looked to a long struggle, after the removal of the "usurpers," between the antagonistic elements concealed within this "people" itself.... But we, too, have been shown to have been wrong by history, which has revealed our point of view of that time to have been an illusion.

[*In partibus (infidelium)—in the midst of the infidels, and so government that exists only on paper].[19]

Elsewhere in the preface, Engels writes why history put them in the wrong: [History] 'made it clear that the state of economic development on the Continent at that time was not, by a long way, ripe for the removal of capitalist production.' [20] Engels writes also about the middle—sections—classes and their growing 'negative' role in the class struggle:

> *An insurrection with which all sections of the people sympathise, will hardly recur; in the class struggle all the middle sections will never group themselves round the proletariat so exclusively that the reactionary parties gathered round the bourgeoisie well-nigh disappear. The "people," therefore, will always appear divided, and with this a powerful lever, so extraordinarily effective in 1848, is lacking.* [21]

The foregoing quotations prove beyond any doubt that Marx's and Engels' theory of classes was drawn up and revised according to economical and political developments in capitalist society. Since Marx and Engels mainly focussed on the most developed form of capitalist society in France, Germany and England during 1845 and 1895, we have to draw up a new analysis of classes when we are studying a writer and his or her literary product in a different country and epoch. We will stay on track of developing a Marxist literary theory by knowing Marx's and Engels' criteria in distinguishing classes.

Marx's and Engels' first criterion in distinguishing classes is **people's—non-ownership of the means of social production.** They distinguished the main class antagonism between the bourgeoisie; 'owners of the means of social production and employers of wage labour' and 'the proletariat, the class of modern wage-labourers who, having no means of production of their own, are reduced to selling their labour power in order to live.'[22] The proletariat was for Marx and Engels the revolutionary class that would bring down the bourgeoisie and its capitalist mode of production and guide society's transition to socialism because the proletarians, 'have nothing of their own to secure and fortify; their mission is to destroy all previous securities for and insurances of, individual property.' [23]

Regarding agriculture, Marx and Engels noted the penetration of capital in its mode of production and they recognized a gradual transformation of peasant and landlord into farm worker and capitalist farmer. This development, however, was in its initial stage during Marx's and Engels' lifetime. The majority of Euope's agricultural population continued their pre-capitalist existence. Marx writes about the French peasants: 'in so far as there exists only a local connection among these farmers, a connection which the individuality and exclusiveness of their interests prevent from generating among them unity of interest, national connections, and political organization, they do not substitute a class.' [24] This lack of 'unity of interest' at local-national level and the absence of a political organisation among the peasants can be positively converted into the second criterion to distinguish classes: **people's collective identification, at local and national level, of their mutual interests that finds its expression in their political organisation.**

Despite 'the increase in numbers of the middle classes' that Marx foresaw, he and Engels didn't make any systematic distinctions between the various sections of the middle class because they considered this class to be conservative and reactionary:

> *The lower middle class, the small manufacturer, the shopkeeper, the artisan, the peasant, all these fight against the bourgeoisie, to save from extinction their existence as fractions of the middle class. They are therefore not revolutionary, but conservative. Nay more, they are reactionary, for they try to roll back the wheel of history. If by chance they are revolutionary, they are so only in view of their impending transfer into the proletariat, they thus defend not their present, but their future interests,...* [25]

There are two 'classes' that Marx and Engels mention incidentally: the lumpenproletariat and the intelectuals. The lumpenproletariat consists of 'vagabonds, criminals and prostitutes' (*Capital I*, p. 797). In *The 18th Brumaire of Louise Bonaparte*, Marx gives a more lively description: 'ruined and adventurous off-shoots of the bourgeoisie, vagabonds, discharged soldiers, pick-pockets, brothel keepers, beggars' etc. Marx didn't analyse the lumpenproletariat's functioning except for its contribution to Louis Bonaparte's coup d'etat in December 1851. Later in history, Adolf Hitler recruits the lumpenproletariat[f] for his private armies SA (Sturmabteilung) and SS (Shutzstaffel).

Intellectuals are divided by Marx and Engels into conservative and progressive ones. The conservative intellectuals are the ruling class's 'active, conceptive ideologists, who make the formation of the illusions of the class about itself their chief source of livelihood.' [26] The progressive intellectuals come from the ruling class, too, and they reach a communist consciousness by contemplating the proletariat's situation or in the *Manifesto* words: 'in times when the class struggle nears the decisive hour…a portion of the bourgeoisie goes over to the proletariat, and in particular a portion of the bourgeois ideologists, who have raised themselves to the level of comprehending theoretically the historical movement as a whole.' [27]

We can state with certainty that Marx and Engels use people's—revolutionary—political consciousness as a yardstick in describing various classes or sections and individuals of classes. This yardstick is the third Marxist criterion in distinguishing classes: **people's—non-possession of a political consciousness that embraces the revolutionary struggle to establish a genuine classless society.**

In summary, we formulated the following Marxist theses for literary theory:

1. The author and his or her literary work can be subjected, can co-exist with, and possibly revolutionize the dominant ideology.

2. Literary production must be based on a writer's unbiased, truthful and 'Shakespearised' description of social reality including a transparent description of the characters' ideology.

3. The writer's class position ought to be counterbalanced by consideration for his or her unique human character.

We were also able to formulate the next three Marxist criteria to distinguish classes:

1. People's—non-ownership of the means of social production.

2. People's collective identification, at local and national level, of their mutual interests that finds its expression in their political organisation.

3. People's—non-possession of a political consciousness that embraces the revolutionary struggle to establish a genuine classless society.

---

f Using Marxism's first and second criteria in distinguishing classes, we can identify large segments of the lumpenproletariat and middle class as the base of the German fascist party in the 1920s and 1930s. They were practically without any means of social production but shared, at a local and national level, a collective identification of their nationalistic and economic interests and they were organized in the National Socialist Party.

These Marxist theses for literary theory and the Marxist criteria to distinguish classes can be useful as guiding principles, but surely aren't meant to be applied as rigid categories of Marxist theory. We have to follow in the footsteps of Marx and Engels and employ the fundamental concept of dialectics:

> *If...investigation always proceeds from this standpoint (that the world is not to be comprehended as a complex of ready-made things, but as a complex of **processes**) the demand for final solutions and eternal truths ceases once for all; one is always conscious of the necessary limitation of all acquired knowledge, of the fact that it is conditioned by the circumstances in which it was acquired.* [28]

NOTES

1. Karl Marx/ Frederick Engels, Collected Works Volume 5, *The German Ideology*, Moscow, Progress Publishers, 1976, p. 59.

2. Ernest Mandel, *The Place of Marxism in History*, New Jersey, Humanities Press, 1994, p. 25.

3. Karl Marx/ Frederick Engels, *Manifesto of the Communist Party*, Second Revised Edition, Moscow, Progress Publishers, 1986, p. 57.

4. Karl Marx/ Frederick Engels, Collected Works Volume 28, New York, International Publishers, Copyright Progress Publishers, Moscow, 1977, p. 42.

5. Ibid., pp. 42-43.

6. F. Engels, Letter to Minna Kautsky, quoted from 'Marx & Engels *On Literature & Art*, by Lee Baxandall and Stefan Morawski, St. Louis, Missouri, Telos Press, 1973, p. 113.

7. Etienne Balibar/ Pierre Macherey, *On Literature as an Ideological Form*, *Untying the text*, Robert Young, London, Routledge, Reprinted 1990, p. 80.

8. Ibid., p. 80.

9. Ibid., p. 80.

10. Karl Marx/ Frederick Engels, Collected Works Volume 28, New York, International Publishers, Copyright Progress Publishers Moscow, 1986, p. 30 and p. 47.

11. Ibid., p. 46.

12. Eleanor Marx, *Notes on the Frienship of Heine and Marx* (1895), quoted from 'Marx & Engels On Literature & Art', by Lee Baxandall and Stefan Morawski, St. Louis. Missouri, Telos Press, 1973, pp. 148-149.

13. Ibid., F. Engels, 'Letter to Margaret Harkness', (April 1888), pp. 115-116.

14. Ibid., Introduction, p. 31.

15. Karl Marx/ Frederick Engels, *Manifesto of the Communist Party*, Second Revised Edition, Moscow, Progress Publishers, 1976, p. 35.

16. F. Engels, *The Origin of the family, Private Property and the State*, Karl Marx/ Frederick Engels, Collected Works Volume 26, New York, International Publishers, Copyright Progress Publishers Moscow, 1990, p. 203.

17. Karl Marx, 'Theories of Surplus Value', London, Lawrence & Wishart, 1951, p. 368.

18. Karl Marx, *Capital* Volume 3, London, Penguin Books Ltd., 1991, p. 1025.

19. F. Engels, Preface to Karl Marx's *The Class Struggles in France*, p. 13, Marxist Library, Volume 24, New York, International Publishers,

20. Ibid., p. 16.

21. Ibid., p. 24.

22. Karl Marx/ Frederick Engels, *Manifesto of the Communist Party*, Second Revised Edition, Progress Publishers Moscow, 1976, p. 35.

23. Ibid., p. 47.

24. Karl Marx, '18th Brumaire'

25. Karl Marx/ Frederick Engels, *Manifesto of the Communist Party*, Second Revised Edition, Moscow, Progress Publishers, 1976, p. 46.

26. Karl Marx/ Frederick Engels, Collected Works Volume 5, *The German Ideology*, Moscow, Progress Publishers1976, p. 60.

27. Karl Marx/ Frederick Engels, *Manifesto of the Communist Party*, Second Revised Edition, Moscow, Progress Publishers, 1976, p. 46.

28. F. Engels, *Ludwig Feuerbach and the Outcome of Classical German Philosophy*, New York, International Publishers, ninth printing, 1988, p. 45.

3

An Analysis of The Setting Sun

Osamu Dazai wrote his novel *The Setting Sun* in 1947. Dazai's father, one of the wealthiest landowners in Aomori Prefecture, served in both the Lower House and the House of Peers. Osamu Dazai, the penname of Shuji Tsushima, was born on June19, 1909. He was the tenth child in his family, having five older brothers, four older sisters and a younger brother. Seventeen members of the extended Tsushima family, and about the same number of servants lived at the Tsushima home. Two or three years before O. Dazai was born, his family had built a huge mansion with many Western and Japanese-style rooms. In his early childhood, Dazai hardly knew his parents; he was suckled by a nursemaid and brought up by an aunt and a nanny until he went to elementary school. Dazai did well in school and, after graduating from middle school and Hirosaki Higher School (in March 1930), he enrolled in the French Literature Department at Tokyo Imperial University. Dazai withdrew from the university in 1935 without obtaining a degree. Instead of studying seriously, Dazai had used his time for writing, womanizing, drinking, taking drugs and suicide attempts. Dazai, who had started publishing short stories when he was in Higher School, started churning out many stories after he ended his two-year-involvement with the illegal Communist Party in the summer of 1932.

In 1935, Dazai was nominated for the first Akutagawa Ryunoseke Prize (the most prestigious literary prize for Japanese writers) on the basis of two stories; he failed to win the prize because of his image as a drug-addict. His first volume of collected works *The Final Years* was published June 25, 1936. Between 1936 and June 13, 1948—the day when Dazai drowned himself—Dazai had a regular output of works. Nevertheless, he depended on a monthly allowance from his family until two years before he died. Half a year before his lovers suicide with his mistress, Tomie Yamazaki, Dazai's novel *The Setting Sun* had become a bestseller. He left behind his wife and three small children at home, and a baby daughter by a different mistress.

The Setting Sun depicts the disintegration of an aristocratic family in postwar Japan. The novel's main characters are Kazuko, who narrates the story, her mother and her brother Naoji. The story starts with a scene of Kazuko and her mother having breakfast in their Chinese-style home in Izu. Kazuko describes minutely her mother's way of eating soup:

> *We lean slightly over the plate, take up a little soup with the spoon held sideways, and then bring it to our mouth, still holding the spoon sideways. Mother, on the other hand, lightly rests the fingers of her left hand on the edge of the table, sits perfectly upright, holds her face firmly high, and without hardly a glance at her plate, she holds the spoon sideways and darts her spoon into the soup. Then,—you want to use the simile—as lightly and gracefully as a swallow, brings the spoon to her mouth at a right angle and pours the soup between her lips from the spoon's tip. Next, while looking innocently around her, she quickly uses the spoon like a little wing, not spilling a drop of soup nor making the least sound of sipping or clinking the plate. Perhaps, this way of eating doesn't confirm to so-called proper etiquette, but to me it is most charming and really looks genuine. However, being, in Naoji's words a high-class beggar and unable to handle my spoon as lightly and as easily as my mother, I'm forced to give up and bend over the plate and eat in a gloomy way prescribed by proper etiquette.* [1]

From Kazuko's reminiscences in the first two chapters we learn the following facts: Kazuko's father died ten years ago. Kazuko, now twenty-nine years old, had been married, but divorced her husband six years ago. Her younger brother Naoji became absorbed in literature when he was in high school and, in imitation of a writer, he had taken to drugs. While still at the university, he was drafted and sent to an island in the Pacific. On the advice from her younger brother, uncle Wada, Kazuko's mother has to sell her home in Tokyo and dismiss all her servants in November 1945. The next month Kazuko and her mother move into their newly bought Chinese-style house in Izu. This change, from living with servants in a big house in Tokyo, to a life without a single servant, in a small cottage in the country, is devastating for Kazuko's mother, who shows the first symptoms of tuberculosis on the very day when they arrive in Izu.

In the summer of 1946, uncle Wada sent Kazuko's mother a letter telling her that Naoji had returned alive from the South Pacific; before Naoji can be released, he has to be cured from his opium addiction. Furthermore, the uncle informs Kazuko's mother that most of the family capital is gone and that he will hardly be able to support her financially. From then on, Kazuko and her mother start selling their clothes (expensive kimono's) to provide for their living expenses.

In the third chapter, Naoji comes home on a summer evening. His first words of greeting Kazuko are: 'How horrifying! This house is out of taste. You should put out a sign, "Chinese Restaurant Rairaiken, Chow Meins being served."' [2]

That first evening at home, Naoji sits for a moment beside his mother who had taken to bed two or three days before his arrival. He bows his head in away of greeting his mother, springs quickly to his feet again and, after a brief exchange of words with Kazuko, he leaves for the village inn to drink. Naoji comes home late that night, and at his mother's request, sleeps between his mother and sister. The next day in the afternoon Naoji gets money from his mother and he goes to meet his friends in Tokyo. He will be absent from home for several weeks. Some days after Naoji's depature, Kazuko wanders in the room where Naoji's clothes, books and other belongings are put away. She picks up one of Naoji's notebooks and starts reading it:

> *To settle a debt of a thousand yen with five yen; it's no laughing matter but that seems to be my approximate effective strength. Rather than people who criticize me by saying, 'Decadent! That must be the only way for you to survive,' I am more thankful to those who tell me to die. Thus, it's expressed clearly. But people seldom say 'Die!' The narrow-minded, calculating hypocrites.... Justice? That's not the essence of the so-called class struggle. Morality? You must be kidding. I know it very well. It's bringing down your fellow-man for the sake of your own happiness: it's a matter of killing. What's the meaning of it, unless there is a verdict of 'Die!' You shouldn't cheat. However our class doesn't have any decent people either. Idiots, apparitions, misers, mad dogs, braggarts, high falutin words, piss from above the clouds. Such people aren't even worthy of being told 'Die!' War. Japan's war is an act of desperation. I won't have it to die by being dragged into an act of desperation. I'd rather die by my own hand.*[3]

Having read some parts in Naoji's notebook, Kazuko thinks back about her divorce, Naoji's drug addiction and her meeting with Naoji's friend, the novelist Mr. Uehara. While married, Kazuko used to let her servant deliver money for Naoji at Mr. Uehara's apartment. Once she went over there herself to meet him personally. Hearing that Kazuko was Naoji's sister, Mr. Uehara asked her to go for a drink. In a building's basement behind the Tokyo Theater, they found a drinking-den and, while having a couple of drinks, they talked about Naoji, drugs and liquor. On the way out from the drinking-den, Mr. Uehara suddenly turned around and kissed Kazuko quickly. Then he hauled a taxi for Kazuko and they didn't meet again untill six years later.

That summer, Naoji being on and off at home, and her mother's illness progressing slowly, Kazuko writes three love letters to Mr. Uehara, stating her desire to make love with him for the purpose of conceiving a child. Her letters aren't answered, and while Kazuko makes up her mind to visit Mr. Uehara, her mother's condition suddenly gets worse. With Kazuko, Naoji and a nurse at her bedside, the mother dies on an autumn day. Kazuko and Naoji then start their life together. Naoji sells all his mother's jewelry on the pretext of getting the necessary capital for his publishing venture in Tokyo, but he uses this money to drink heavily in Tokyo. One day Naoji comes home in Izu with a girl who looks like a dancer. Kazuko seizes this opportunity to leave for Tokyo, where she heads straight for Mr. Uehara's home. Mrs. Uehara answers the door because her husband is out drinking. Kazuko's shoe's strap is broken and Mrs. Uehara invites Kazuko inside. She gives Kazuko a new leather strap to replace the broken one and tells Kazuko where to find her husband.

That evening Kazuko finds Mr. Uehara in a bar called 'Chidori'. He's drinking like a fish in the company of about ten people. Three of them are girls who drink and smoke like the men. When Mr. Uehara notices Kazuko entering, he motions her to sit beside him and without exchanging a word, Mr. Uehara pours her a glass of liquor, fills his own glass and he says in a hoarse, low voice 'Cheers!' After a while Kazuko goes to the next room and is invitited by the bar's madam to eat noodles with her and the maid. After having drunk enough, Mr. Uehara comes into the room, too, and he proposes to guide Kazuko to his friend's house where she can sleep. On the way to Mr. Uehara's friend's place, Kazuko and Mr. Uehara engage in a long conversation, from which I will take a few excerpts.

'Have you read my letters? [Kazuko] 'Yes.' 'What's your answer?' 'I hate the aristocracy. After all, there is something detestably arrogant about them. Your brother Naoji, though a great succes as an aristocrat, sometimes displays an affectation that I can't stand. I'm a farmer's son from the country-side and when passing a stream like this one, I always wearily remember my childhood days. I used to fish for carp or scoop up Killifishes in the stream in my hometown'... 'Do you still love me?' His voice was rough. 'Do you want a child from me?' I didn't answer. His face approached mine with the power of a rockslide and he furiously kissed me. The kisses reeked of sexual desire. I wept while accepting them. Bitter tears, like tears of defeat and regret kept pouring from my eyes.

Near daybreak at Mr. Uehara's friends home:

Before I was aware of it, he was lying next to me. For almost an hour I maintained a frantic resistance of silence. Suddenly I felt sorry for him and yielded.... That morning my brother Naoji committed suicide.

Kazuko's statement about her brother's suicide is followed by Naoji's testament:

Dear sister,

It's no use, I'm going first. I cannot think of any reason why I should have to go on living....
I am better off dead. I don't have the so-called capacity for living. I don't have the strength to quarrel with people over money. I can't even sponge on people. When I went drinking with Mr. Uehara I always paid my share of the bill. Mr. Uehara called that my cheap aristocrat's pride, which he really hated. However, I didn't pay out of pride: I absolutely couldn't drink, eat or hold a woman with money that Mr. Uehara had earned.[6]

In the last half of the testament, Naoji describes in a fictional way—without mentioning proper names and profession—his love for a painter's wife. From the circumstantial description, it's immediately obvious that Naoji means the wife of the writer Mr. Uehara. His love for her remained platonic, but Naoji often went to visit Mr. Uehara, who he describes as an uneducated, unreliable and squalid man, in the hope of meeting Mr. Uehara's wife. Naoji's testament ends: 'Once more good-bye. Kazuko, I am, after all, an aristocrat.'[7]

The Setting Sun's final chapter consists of Kazuko's last letter to Mr. Uehara. About one month after Naoji's suicide, when she knows to be pregnant with Mr. Uehara's child, she writes the following:

It seems that you too have abandoned me; no, you are gradually forgetting me. But I am happy. I have gotten pregnant as I wanted.... Recently, I have come to understand why war, peace, unions, politics exist in the world. I don't suppose you know. That's why you will be unhappy forever. I will tell you why: it is that women give birth to healthy babies.... I no longer want to tell you flimsy, perfunctory remarks, such as stop drinking, cure your illness, lead a long life, do splendid work etc. Perhaps you will earn the gratitude of future generations more by recklessly pursuing your life of vice than by your splendid work. Victims. Victims of a transitional period of morality; that's what we both are for sure. Where on earth is the revolution carried out? Around us still persists the old morality, which doesn't break apart and blocks our path. No matter how much the waves on the sea's surface may rage, the water at the bottom, far from being moved by revolution, lies motionless and 'pretends' to be asleep. However I think of having pushed the old morality slightly aside in my first struggle. I intend to similarly fight a second and third struggle together with the child who will be born.... A victim is the most beautiful thing in the present world. There was another little victim. Mr. Uehara. I don't feel like asking anything more of you, but for that little victim, grant me only one favor. I would like your wife to hold my child in her arms, even once will do, and at that time let me say, 'Naoji secretely had this child from a certain woman.'

An Analysis Of *The Setting Sun*

The first scene, Kazuko's mother eating soup, presents a Marxist approach in analysing literature with insurmountable problems. It would be ridiculous to relate 'eating soup' with the dominant ideology; the same can be said about the way of eating soup: a beggar can eat like a queen and a queen can eat like a beggar. A transparant description of Kazuko's mother's ideology and or a consideration of Dazai's class position regarding 'eating soup' will take us into cloud-cuckoo-land. On the other hand, Dazai differentiates between two members of the aristocracy, Kazuko and her mother, according to their eating style. He describes Kazuko as a high-class beggar and her mother as a real aristocrat. This differentiating between members of the same class isn't completely lacking in Marxist Theory (conservative opposed to progressive intellectuals), but 'eating style' isn't a Marxist criteria for differentiating. Kazuko's choice—struggle—in the end of the story, to fight the old morality by getting pregnant, also doesn't fit anywhere in Marxist Theory and Practice. In a confrontation between Marxist Theory and literature, 'Kazuko's mother way of eating soup' and 'Kazuko's choice of getting pregnant', brings to light the weakness of the Marxist class concept. Instead of Marxist Theory, it's literature that provides a better, more realistic understanding of differentiating class members and a way of fighting the old morality.

The second quotation is the raving of a ruined, drug-addicted off-shoot of the aristocracy. Dazai might have belonged to the progressive intellectuals during his two-year-involvement with the illegal Japanese Communist Party (1930–1932); by the time when *The Setting Sun* was published in 1947, Dazai had become a celebrated writer and he still might have been sympathetic toward a revolutionary struggle, but surely he wouldn't have supported a revolution instigated by a communist party with the purpose of establishing a socialist society. In the story *Tokatonton*, published in January 1947, Dazai writes about the 22nd general election held on 10 April 1946:

People were talking about democracy and whatnot in this year's April general election, but I don't trust them. The Liberal and Progressive parties were unchanged and old-fashioned. The Socialist and Communist parties were elated and took advantage of the defeat in war which had given them a chance to become active.

> *Likewise, it gave the filthy impression of unconditional surrender's corpse infested with worms—an impression I can't forget.*[9]

Dazai was definitely displeased with the established political order and even more so with the Socialist and Communist parties. We also have to observe that Dazai didn't consider 'justice' to be the essence of the class struggle: in the following quotation Dazai conveys his political ideas by describing Kazuko's experience reading Rosa[a] Luxemburg's book, *Introduction to Economics:*

> *If it is read as economics, it's really boring.... However, reading the book I felt a singular excitement for a different reason. The author goes along with daredevil courage destroying the conventional ideas one after another, without the slightest hesitation.... Destructive ideas. Destruction is pathetic and sorrowful and this is beautiful. The dream of destroying, building anew, perfecting. Although if a a person has once destroyed, the day of completion may never come, nevertheless, because of my yearning for love, I have to destroy. I must start a revolution.* [10]

In the foregoing chapter, I formulated three Marxist criteria to distinguish classes. Regarding Dazai and *The Setting Sun* let us review the hardest applicable third criterion: People's—non-possession of a political consciousness. Dazai certainly has a political consciousness that embraces the revolutionary struggle to establish a genuine classless society: but how to deal with Dazai's strong antipathy to politicians and the Socialist and Communist parties? Dazai's description of destroying and building anew is coincidentally the same as the German philosopher Nietzsche's: 'The desire for destruction, change and becoming can be an expression of an overflowing energy that is pregnant with future...'[11]

Although Dazai can be considered as a progressive intellectual—During the Pacific War, the Japanese censors kept a wary eye on Dazai and publishers became more reluctant to ask him for manuscripts[12]—his character Naoji provides us the answer why Dazai wouldn't be considered a 'progressive intellectual' from a Marxist viewpoint: 'Once more good-bye. Kazuko, I am, after all, an aristocrat.'

Aristocrats will remain aristocrats their whole life, even during and after revolutions, because aristocrats aren't improvised: they are the fruit of a special social environment. Marx, Engels and Lenin were from aristocratic families, too, and notwithstanding their brilliant insights into economics, politics etc., I strongly doubt their ability to understand diverse human characters within the **various classes:** especially they didn't understand what 'usual' people do understand; so far, Marxist Theory has been far more readily consumed by bourgeois intellectuals than by the broad working masses.

Now we have come to a somewhat strange situation: Dazai, a Japanese writer from an aristocratic family, has a better understanding of himself and of the diverse human characters within his own class than Marx and Engels did; Dazai knew he was an aristocrat and, because of this, he would never be able to become one of the proletariat. This knowledge led to his first suicide attempt when he was 19 years old. Dazai writes about this incident in an essay entitled *An Almanac of Agony:*

> *All the rich people were bad. All the aristocrats were bad. Rightneous belonged only to the poor, humble masses. I was for the armed insurrection. A revolution without the quillotine was meaningless. However, I was not one of the poor, humble masses. My role in this would be to submit to the quillotine. I was a nineteen-year-old higher school student. In my class, I alone wore gorgeous clothes. Really, there was nothing left for me but to die. I swallowed a large quantity of Calmotin* [a sleeping medicine], *but I didn't die.*[13]

---

[a] Rosa Luxemburg (1871–1919), Polish and German revolutionary. She was murdered by right-wing officers during a revolutionary uprising in Berlin, 1919.

The Marxist concept that 'a portion of the bourgeoisie will go over to the proletariat...and in particular a portion of the bourgeois ideologists, who have raised themselves to the level of comprehending theoretically the historical movement as a whole...' [14] isn't wrong, but it veils the simple reality that in the end, a bourgeois ideologist can't become one of the proletariat.

The third quotation 'To settle a debt of a thousand yen...' conveys several clearly stated opinions: Dazai (and or his character Naoji) prefers to be told the truth bluntly; the class struggle's essence isn't justice; Japan's war is an act of desperation etc. Many common Japanese people might have shared Dazai's ideas, especially about Japan's war, but this last idea would have been strongly condemned by Japan's military leaders who were in control of Japan from 1932 until 1945. Dazai could safely express this idea in 1947, because the war had ended in defeat and disaster. Dazai wasn't subjected anymore to the dominant ideology of a Japanese military regime.

Another unique, unusual Dazai idea is expressed in the following sentence: 'I won't have it to die by being dragged into an act of desperation, I'd rather die by my own hand.' Normally, a forty-year-old man might say: 'I won't have it to die for my country, I'd rather **stay alive** for my family.' Dazai often chose his way out of problems by suicide attempts and in 'imitating' his character Naoji; he committed suicide one year later, leaving behind his wife and three children and a child by a mistress.

The choice of suicide—like Kazuko's choice of getting pregnant—is very fundamental and can't be discounted only by moral and religious values. I don't think these 'choices' can be adequately explained from the concept of ideology: the will to live and die are closely connected with the 'reason' of mankind's existence. From the very beginning, this reason must have been an integral component of language (literature), because language constitutes itself as the motive force of men's history.

Kazuko's narrating how she yielded to Mr. Uehara by feeling sorry, seems to contradict her fervent wish of getting pregnant, but fits with a trend in the 1990s of more people wanting to have children without being married and sometimes without sex. Dazai was, at this point, able to fight—revolutionize—the old morality. Likewise, Naoji's choice of committing suicide presents a fight against the old morality (morality to be considered as a part of ideology).

Besides revolutionizing the dominant ideology, Dazai 'recreates' an idea of universal and permanent interest: intentionally ending and creating life. Dazai processes this idea uniquely by letting Naoji commit suicide the same morning his sister conceives a child. 'Coincidentally', Kazuko conceives a child from the husband whose wife Naoji is in love with. In Kazuko's last letter, Dazai gives an unbiased, truthful and 'Shakespearised' description of social reality: war and peace exist for the purpose of 'women giving birth to healthy babies'. Kazuko has sex solely to get pregnant. She fights the old morality by becoming a single parent.

Though, on the surface, Dazai and his literature complies with the Marxist theses for literary theory (revolutionize dominant ideology; unbiased, truthful etc. description of social reality; class position counterbalanced by suicide attempts): Kazuko's ideas and concrete solutions are fundamentally different from Marxist Theory and Practice.

For example Engels considering sex love: 'that personal beauty, intimate association, similarity in inclinations, etc., aroused desire for sexual intercourse among people of opposite sexes'[15] which idea Engels foresaw to be developed and realised in the near future: this idea of individual sex love is completely absent in Kazuko's calculated 'surrender' to Mr. Uehara's sexual desire.

Marx's and Engels' ideas, such as: 'The care and upbringing of the children becomes a public affair.'[16] '...we replace home education by social.'[17] 'The bourgeois clap-trap about the family and education, about the hallowed co-relation of parent and child, becomes all the more disgusting, by the action of Modern Industry, all family ties among the proletarians are torn asunder and their children transformed into simple articles of commerce, and instruments of labour.'[18] All these ideas clash with Kazuko's progressive aristocratic ideas. Notwithstanding this clash, Dazai provides transparant descriptions of his characters' ideology; he exposes the decay of his own class against the background of his country's 'desperate' war.

We know that Marx and Engels don't judge a literary work according to 'reactionary' or 'progressive' class values that are incarnated in it, which leads us to Kazuko's 'pessimistic' ideas about revolution. She sees around her a bastion of old morality that doesn't stir and blocks progress. However Kazuko's description of herself as 'a victim of a transitional period of morality', acknowledges a changing morality: the aristocracy's morality is disintegrating and vanishing. Kazuko's progessive aristocratic values are born of the aristocrats' decay. Dazai's sympathies are all with the class doomed to extinction (*Compare* Engels opinion about Balzac).

Could we have demanded a more 'socialist' or 'revolutionary' orientated work from Dazai? Such a demand would be acceptable when the writer had chosen to write for the political enlightnement of his or her readers, but Dazai's purpose to write *The Setting Sun* couldn't have been political, or he surely would have mentioned the tremendous influence of the Occupation Personnel under command of general Douglas MacArthur that were stationed in Japan from 1945 until 1952. Knowing that Dazai's purpose wasn't political, we ought to abandon the foregoing demand for a more 'socialist' or 'revolutionary' orientated work.

Concluding, we have observed Dazai's technique of differentiating (which equals Marx's 'Shakespearising') that might be useful for Marxist Theory to precise its definitions of classes; Dazai's understanding of the very limited role that an aristocrat can play in a socialist revolution (which understanding could have been useful for Russian, Chinese and Cuban revolutionaries). We also observed that Dazai revolutionized the dominant ideology and recreated the important themes of intentionally ending and creating life. In the end we noticed that Dazai didn't write *The Setting Sun* with a political purpose in mind and, therefore we shouldn't demand a more 'socialist' or 'revolutionary' orientated novel. From this last observation and Engels' distinction between the novel and the socialist tendentious novel, I deduce the fourth Marxist thesis for literary theory: 4. When analysing a literary work we have to account, if possible, for which purpose it was written.

Summary of all the theses about mechanisms at work in literature:

1. The writer processes his or her thoughts, feelings, impressions, echoes that emanate from his or her life in a functioning society, into a literary product.

2. The writer's main tool 'language knowledge' has been largely set and predetermined.

3. Language functions have a consumptive as well as a productive nature, which may interrelate, influence and run over into each other.

4. Language functions form a unity in variety that through the writer are fused into an organic literary product.

5. Literary production is subjected to the market mechanisms of present capitalistic society; it has to turn out a profit.

6. A literary product can't be something completely new or unique, although processed through the writer in a unique form or style, expressing ideas of permanent or universal interest, it may provide artistic joy to mankind for centuries.

7. A writer brings unintentional meanings, motives and understandings into his or her literary work.

8. From different viewpoints—psychological, social-political, historical etc.—we can establish different interpretations of a literary work.

9. While a writer uses various techniques—choice of discourse and speech type—bases his or her writing on different production processes: it's the contrast between the discourse carrier and the public moral values for the various meanings that has to be the essenttial ingredient of his or her literature.

10. Class-struggle influences language.

11. Language (ideological language) influences class struggle.

12. Incorrectly signifying meaning is the source of the disunity between material-social activity and language.

13. By exposing unintentional meanings, motives and understandings that a writer brings into his or her literary work; defining my viewpoint; exposing the writer's viewpoint; framing the writer and his or her liter-

ary work in a social-historical context, I can recognize a unified text with a determinate meaning.

14. Multi-language consciousness operates inside the writer and his or her literary work.

15. When using personal experience and thought as the basis of a literary work, a writer can portray an event on the same time-and-value plane as his or her contemporaries.

16. A literary work is in contact with every day life and the domains of philosophy, religion etc.

17. The concept of 'A Cry Of The Soul' springs up from a literary's work's contents, but to produce this 'cry' we will have to use Osamu Dazai's method: 'It seemed the only way was to suddenly grasp, without question what is simple, natural and clear and put it directly on paper...'

18. Movement enforcements establish the narrative with its meanings and values.

19. The 'third person' as created in the character of the rogue, clown, fool or recreated by the writer in the 'I' character of himself or herself inside the story corresponds to a quasi character's discourse in which the authorial viewpoint is cloaked in the character's discourse.

20. The author and his or her literary work can be subjected, can co-exist with, and possibly revolutionize the dominant ideology.

21. Literary production must be based on a writer's unbiased, truthful and Shakespearised' description of social reality including a transparant description of the characters' ideology.

22. The writer's class position ought to be counterbalanced by consideration for his or her unique human character.

23. When analysing a literary work we have to account, if possible, for which purpose it was written.

NOTES

1. Osamu Dazai, *Shayo* (*The Setting Sun*), *Shayo-Ningen Shikkaku*, Tokyo, Shinchosha, 1979, p. 8. Translated by W. Nuyten.

2. Ibid., p. 38.

3. Ibid., p. 43.

4. Ibid., p. 89.

5. Ibid., p. 90.

6. Ibid., pp. 94-100.

7. Ibid., p. 100.

8. Ibid., pp. 100-101.

9. Ibid., *Tokatonton*, p. 235, Translated by L. Perkins.

10. Ibid., *Shayo,* Translated by W. Nuyten.

11. Friedrich Nietzsche, (original title: *Die Fröliche Wissenschaft) The Gay Science*, translated by Walter Kaufmann, New York, Vintage Books, Copyright 1974 by Random House, Inc., p. 329.

12. Osamu Dazai, *Self Portraits,* Translated and introduced by Ralp F. McCarthy, Tokyo–New York–London, Kodansha International, 1992, p. 21.

13. Osamu Dazai, *Kuno no Nenkan (An Almanac of Agony)*, *Ningenshikkaku*, Tokyo, Shinchosha, 1979, pp. 191-192. Translated by W. Nuyten.

14. Karl Marx/ Frederick Engels, *Manifesto of the Communist Party*, Moscow, Second Revised Edition, Progress Publishers, 1976, p. 46.

15. F. Engels, *The Origin of the Family, Private Property and the State*, Karl Marx/ Frederick Engels, Collected Works 26, New York, International Publishers, Copyright Progress Publishers Moscow, 1990, p. 183.

16. Ibid., p. 183.

17. Karl Marx/ Frederick Engels, *Manifesto of the Communist Party*, Moscow, Second Revised Edition, Progress Publishers, p. 55.

18. Ibid., p. 55.

Appendix A

Interview with Karl Marx: Engelsism

Preface

A few months ago, I got a big wooden box my family had sent by boat. My brother Matthew had written me that some of our great grandfather, Henricus Huysmans, old documents had been found in the attic after our grandmother died. Matthew wrote, "We're sending these old, yellowed, literary remnants to you because no one else in the family is interested in them."

I remembered only that Henricus Huysmans had been a writer for a provincial Dutch newspaper.

Unable to control my curiosity, when I got the box, I opened it immediately. Although the papers were old and slightly yellow, they were in good condition. There were several volumes of poems, many volumes of essays about social problems, and at the bottom was a big, brown envelope with the words, "This Material Is Censored and Can't Be Used." I opened the envelope and took out ten notebooks. When I saw the titles, I couldn't believe my eyes. The notebooks had such titles as *Interview with Kropotkin*, *Interview with Liebknecht* and *Interview with F. Engels*. Two notebooks were entitled *Interview with Karl Marx*. These notebooks, carefully handwritten in pen, contained the accounts of four conversations Henricus Huysmans had with Karl Marx. My great grandfather had written down the account in Dutch. Here is my English translation of the first of four conversations.

Alexander Huysmans

Mishima, Japan, 1996

H. Huysmans: I'm glad to be on solid earth again. The boat trip from Holland to England really shook up my insides. Here on solid earth, surrounded by your collection of thousands of books, I'm starting to recover my strength.

K. Marx: It's too bad we couldn't meet on the continent. Unfortunately, the waves of reactionary hatred, which roared up around me in Germany, France and Belgium, forced me to the coast of England. The books, which have partly contributed to your recovery, don't belong to my private collection. Most of them are borrowed and many belong to my friend Engels.*

H. Huysmans: You mentioned waves of reactionary hatred, but before we go into that, I'd like to give prospective readers of my book some information about your youth, upbringing, and the like.

K. Marx: There are more important subjects to talk about than my youth, but for the reading public – don't forget to ask a good, timely price for your book – I'll do what you ask.

H. Huysmans: What do you mean a "timely" price?

K. Marx: Your publisher is a businessman, isn't he? He'll try to keep his printers' pay, like your share, as low as he can so he'll get more profit. Your publisher will have expenses in the beginning, but you won't be paid your share until almost one year after the book goes on sale. Your publisher will get interest on your share during this time. That's why I mentioned a "timely" price. You should get the interest on your share.

H. Huysmans: I follow your reasoning, but if my book doesn't sell well or doesn't sell at all, the publisher will have a big loss.

K. Marx: An efficient businessman knows his market. Also, if you print this interview with me – Karl Marx, the most feared advocate of the international working class – like an introductory article to your book, your publisher and you will be sure to make money.

Let me now get back to the subject of my youth. I was born on the fifth of May 1818, in Trier. My cradle was covered with the best quality lace and silk, since my parents were well off. My mother Henriette was a Dutch Jewess, who throughout her life had struggled with the German language. My father,

Morchedaï Marx, descended from a family of rabbis. He was the first in his family to give up studying the Talmud and he became a lawyer. I was six years old when my father decided to baptize the family. Consequently, I became a Christian German Jew with Dutch blood in my veins.

H. Huysmans: In your youth did you ever feel rebellious toward your parents?

K. Marx: No, absolutely not. We lived in a big, beautiful house in Trier, where my sisters and I had a happy-go-lucky childhood. After I graduated from the gymnasium (secondary school), my father gave me the freedom and financial support for my university studies. The first year I studied at the University of Bonn. On my father's advice, the next four years I studied at the bigger, more serious University of Berlin. In 1841, I got my doctorate in philosophy with a dissertation about Epicurus' philosophy.

H. Huysmans: Your ambition was to start working in philosophy, wasn't it?

K. Marx: Yes, I planned to get a professorship and to get a source of income for my upcoming marriage. This plan quickly fell through because the Prussian government started banning liberal-minded philosophers like me from working at universities. As you know, in those days we had an absolutist monarchy that didn't recognize suffrage, freedom of the press, or human rights.

H. Huysmans: After you realized you couldn't work at a university, what did you do?

K. Marx: I was twenty-four and it was time for me to independently earn my bread. A progressive newspaper, *Rheinische Zeitung*, established that year in Cologne, had an opening for me as a contributor. My philosophical background was helpful in writing articles dealing with social problems of the day. I was soon promoted to editor-in-chief and faced the future fully confident. In that same year, 1842, my friend Engels also contributed regularly to our paper.

H. Huysmans: You mentioned your friend Engels. In studying your writings, I noticed that Engels greatly influenced the ideas you formulated on society.

K. Marx: I have to compliment you for your dilligent study. Your observation is correct. Unlike me, Engels was levelheaded. Philosophy was only a hobby for him – something to do in the evening. In the daytime he worked in his family's textile mill in Manchester. While I wasted my time with minor philosophical problems and fulfilling the role of progressive editor-in-chief in Germany, Engels grasped the meaning of the factory system. He saw the huge profits of the factory owners and the miserable conditions of the workers and their families. He busied himself with concrete living conditions of the new working class and their developing political consciousness. He started analyzing the contemporary economic order from a communist viewpoint. I hadn't progressed very much.

H. Huysmans: To explain to the readers, I'd like to ask you what do the terms 'Communism' and 'Marxism' mean?

K. Marx: Your question is concise. I'm afraid my answer will be somewhat lengthy. Communism is the proletariat's action directed toward establishing a new society. This will only be practically possible if all proletarian classes in the most advanced countries act in unison. These countries must have wealth, culture and a highly developed productive force. We don't want proletarian classes to establish a new society based on poverty and misery. In these countries, the wealth, and especially use of productive forces, is concentrated in the hands of the bourgeoisie. By bourgeoisie I mean the modern capitalistic class – owners of the means of social production and employers of paid labor. The proletariat is the modern paid labor class who don't have any means of production on their own, but are reduced to selling their labor to live. This class, through their labor, bears all the burdens of society without really enjoying the wealth of society. Gradually the proletariat develops an awareness of communism and, possibly; a small minority of the bourgeoisie, by contemplating the proletarian class situation, develops such an awareness. This awareness of communism realizes the need for a basic revolution to abolish the previous class society. Instead of the class society with its antagonisms, we'll have an association where free individual development is a condition for everyone's development.

The second part of the question about the meaning of 'Marxism'* embarrasses me. Others have recently used this term in discussing my worldview. The problem is, I've never developed a complete world view. I didn't have enough time and I thought it was more important to actually contribute to changing the world.

H. Huysmans: Let's go back to the time you were working as editor-in-chief for the *Rheinische Zeitung*. You had a good position and good income, and you were planning to get married. What happened?

K. Marx: I often expressed incisive comments in my articles that weren't very well received by the government. Through censorship, the government closed the paper in March 1843. I understood that my progressiveness was still mired in the marshes of philosophy and decided to broaden my views. I immersed myself in dozens of studies, and although I was out of a job, I married Jenny von Westphalen that summer. She was twenty-nine and I was twenty-five on our wedding day. After thirty-nine years of marriage, she died last year. Sometimes I feel guilty for all the hardships she suffered because she married me. She was of noble birth: her father was Baron Johan Ludwig von Westphalen, and her brother became Prussian Minister of Interior. She had six children, three of whom died while she was alive. Tragic…Still, she never left my side.

H. Huysmans: You have her photograph over there. May I have a closer look at it.?

K. Marx: Sure.

H. Huysmans: She radiates beauty and generosity.

K. Marx: This photograph was taken several weeks after we were married. That summer we lived with Jenny's mother in Kreuznach. The next fall we left for Paris. Together with another émigré German editor, I started working on a new journal.

H. Huysmans: Luckily, I found a copy of that journal in a Parisian bookstore. It was published as a double issue entitled *Deutsch-Französische Jahrbücher* in February 1844. Several authors contributed articles, but I carefully studied your two articles and the two contributions written by Engels. Now, forty years later, can you still remember the contents?

K. Marx: It wouldn't be very easy to quote the exact contents, but I can clearly recall the general tenor. One of my articles dealt with the 'Jewish Question.' I'll dwell on this article in more detail because of my Jewish family background.

The philosopher Bruno Bauer had rejected freeing German Jews for two reasons: First, the Jews weren't willing to free themselves from their imagined Jewish nationality. Second, the Germans themselves lived under an oppressive regime. In my article I disagreed with Bauer that Jews had to rid themselves of Judaism—religion is ultimate private. Also, Bauer had pointed out the contradiction that, without having political rights, the Jews still had enormous power and political influence on society. I endorsed this view and added that politically freeing the Jews wasn't important—what was important was freeing mankind. As you know, money is God to the Jews, and money has become God to the world. The Jews taught the Christians—the Dutch and Belgians included—to worship money. Money is the jealous God of Israel, in the face of which no other gods are allowed to exist. I have a coin here that represents the value of gold to you, but you forget that a certain amount of labor was required to produce this coin. The value of this coin is based on the human labor that went into its production. This coin and the notes issued by the banks we call money, and man worships money. From a social viewpoint, money is the diverted essence of man's labor. As soon as society abolishes Judaism—huckstering and selling to make money and its preconditions—Jews can no longer exist because they won't have any object in the form of money. Socially freeing the Jew means freeing society from Judaism. You shouldn't think I'm anti-Semitic or anti-bourgeoisie; the Jews and the bourgeoisie themselves are social products of the social economic structure. From a more personal viewpoint, as a German Jew with Dutch blood, I can't be held responsible for the autocratic Prussian government, money Judaism and the Dutch slave trade and colonial exploitation of the Dutch West Indies.

H. Huysmans: An interesting book entitled *Max Havelaar* by Eduard Douwes Dekker, was published about exploiting the Dutch West Indies. If you have time, I suggest you read it.

K. Marx: Have time? Really, where would I find the time. But, don't let me get of the subject. My other contribution to the *Deutsch-Französische Jahrbücher* dealt with the problem of human freedom. Gradually I advanced one pace. I concluded that material force is necessary to overthrow material force, but the theory also becomes a material force as soon as it grips the masses.

H. Huysmans: You made high-level contributions, but…

K. Marx: I know what you're going to say, but still Friedrich Engels' contributions were better! You ought to know that Friedriech Engels was a born Marxist. Ha, ha, now I use this unjustified term myself. It would be better to use ENGELSISM instead of Marxism. He was the one who showed the way, figuratively and literally, and for the greater part he has paid this way.

H. Huysmans: I have studied Engels' articles in the *Deutsch-Französische Jahrbücher* and I'll try to summarize his most important article, *Outlines of a Critique of Political Economy*. He described all the economic theories and their shortcomings. According to Engels, the big mistake with economics was that it didn't question the validity of private property. Economics has turned the world topsy-turvy. The term 'national wealth' doesn't have any meaning as long as there is private property. The English 'national wealth' is great, but they're the poorest people under the sun. Engels remarks about the rent theory that the landowner who doesn't sow, reaps. Economists can't understand or explain the opposition and relations between competition and monopoly, labor and capital, overproduction and crises. Engels concludes that competition sets capital against capital, labor against labor, landed property against landed property, and each against the other two. Labor is the weakest competitor in the struggle with capital and landed property; the worker has to work to live, while the landowner can live on his rent and the capitalist can survive on his interest or on his capital and property.

On the internal competition of labor, capital and landed property, Engels says that the stronger worker drives the weaker worker out of the market, just as the bigger capital absorbs the smaller capital and the bigger landed property absorbs the smaller landed property. These developments in present society will result in centralizing property and in times of crises in trade and agriculture, centralization will accelerate. Engels ends his article with the Engelsistic remark that this centralization trend can be stopped only by fusing opposing interests and doing away with private property.

K. Marx: You gave an excellent summary. Yes, that article was a sublime contribution from Engels. It started influencing my thoughts. A year later, in 1845, Engels supplemented that article with information from economists, sociologists, historians and working class newspapers and rewrote it into his famous book *The Condition of the Working Class in England.* My respect for that book is no secret. In my life work *Das Kapital,* I wrote how well Engels understood the spirit of the capitalist production mode. The genius in his book is borne out by comparing his work with official government reports about factories and mines that appear in publications twenty years after Engels' book. In particular, compared with the official reports of the Children's Employment Commission, published eighteen to twenty years after Engels' book was published, confirm, in detail, conditions Engels depicts of how the working class lived and worked. It describes the exploiting and barbaric treatment of women and children in working day and night, death by starvation, factory accidents, rising criminality, disgusting housing, cholera and destruction of family life. These details about workers' living conditions were described from the development of the capitalist production mode.

Engels was the first person to make the connection between the industrial revolution and development of communist awareness in the working class. From Engels I learned to change from abstract philosophy to studying real people, their activities and their material living conditions.

H. Huysmans: In February 1845, the French police ordered you to leave the country. Could you briefly explain this being expelled?

K. Marx: Those were hard times. With a wife and a child, almost broke, I suddenly had to leave the country. I was expelled because of my contributions to the newspaper *Vorwärts*, a paper that came out twice a week, with readers in Paris and in Germany. Heinrich Börnstein, the founder and editor of *Vorwärts,* gratefully accepted contributions from the Russian anarchist Bakoenin, the German poets Heinrich Heine and Georg Herwegh, and the disinherited Jewish merchant's son Moses Hess—who had transformed himself into a radical writer. Just name them—beautiful company!

In their *Vorwärts* contributions, the German émigrés mercilessly and cuttingly criticized the Prussian government and her king, Friedrich Wilhelm the Fourth. It didn't take long for a reaction. At the request of the Prussian government, the French minister Guizot ordered all *Vorwärts* contributors to leave the country within five weeks. Thus at the beginning of February, I got to Brussels where I could stay for three years.

H. Huysmans: I read in newspaper articles that you came to and left Belgium under unfriendly, hostile conditions. Could you tell me about your arrival, your three-year stay, and your leaving Brussels?

K. Marx: Well, when I got there, I had to sign a deposition that I wouldn't publish anything about Belgium's current politics. During my three years in Belgium, I wrote various books, of which I wrote *The German Ideology* with Engels. I wrote my first economical book *The Poverty of Philosophy* in French and, Engels and I also wrote *The Manifesto of the Communist Party*, which was first published in London in 1848.

In Brussels, Engels and I met the other German émigrés and we contacted working-class movement participants in Paris and London.

At the end of February 1848, a revolution, enthusiastically welcomed by the Belgian working class, broke out in Paris. The reaction this time was swift. Within two days all German émigrés were arrested and expelled from the country. After spending one night in a Brussels' prison, on March fifth I got to Paris, which was overpowered by the revolution.

H. Huysmans: As I concluded from the introduction to *The Manifesto of the Communist Party*, this booklet was written as a theoretical and practical Communist League platform. Could you, from misty veiled history, explain something about the origin of this League and you and Engels joining this League?

K. Marx: For the league's origin, we have to look to France. In the middle of the thirties, a group of German émigrés had formed 'The League of the Just' in France.

After a revolt in Paris, during which city hall was occupied for a couple of hours, it was soon evident that a few members of 'The League of the Just' had taken part. These members were arrested and expelled from France. among them was Karl Schapper, who left for London and, with six like-minded people, founded the Communist League.

This League, which worked with vague convictions and without a well-defined platform, began to recognize its own weakness. The League learned about Engels' and my writings, our work for the various political and working-class organizations in Brussels. A League representative, Joseph Moll, came to visit Engels and me in Brussels and asked us to join the League. He made a unique proposal: we were asked to write draft regulations of the League as well as a manifesto to define a clearly-defined platform. We couldn't turn down the proposal and joined the Communist League. At conferences in the summer of 1847 and in November and December 1847, with German, Belgian, French, Swiss and English worker organization representatives present, the regulations Engels and I drew up were accepted and *The Manifesto of the Communist Party* was adopted as the League's official manifesto.

H. Huysmans: As far as I could gather, 1848 and 1849 were stormy years for you and Engels. After staying briefly in Paris, you both went back to Germany, where you founded the paper *Neue Rheinische Zeitung*. Assisted by Engels, with you as editor in chief, you started publishing this paper. Why did you publish this paper in Germany?

K. Marx: A paper written for the German working class and creating a German proletariat mass party were essential to prepare for the class struggle. The paper, which provided a political education for the working class, defended working class interests and inspired them to actively participate in the newly formed workers' organizations. About the time we started publishing the *Neue Rheinishe Zeitung,* the French army, led by minister Cavaignac, crushed the proletarian insurgents in Paris. These Parisian workers revolted June twenty-second because the government hadn't kept the promises made in February that year. With the end of the French revolution by brute armed force, we tried to support the revolutionary mood among the German working class.

H. Huysmans: After some legal prosecution of instigating a revolution, for which you were always acquitted, the Prussian government couldn't put up with your presence. You were a dangerous man in those days.

K. Marx: Although I used only a pen, I was dangerous for the ruling class, that's true. In May 1849, I was ordered to leave the country. After a short stay, my family and I were expelled from Paris, too. In August 1849, on a warm summer day, I got to London. My wife and children followed a month later. Engels, who had taken part in the last revolutionary struggle in Germany, ran the risk of being arrested and, after wandering through Switzerland and Italy, reached London in November 1849 by boat.

H. Huysmans: That was thirty-three years ago. A lot has happened since then. Thank you for your time. I hope we can continue our conversation tomorrow.

K. Marx: As long as you don't ask Marxist questions, you're welcome.

H. Huysmans: No, no. I'll try to keep it Engelsistic.

HENRICUS HUYSMANS, LONDON

26 December 1882

NOTES

*The short story doesn't provide information about Friedrich Engels' childhood, but he was the oldest son of a German bourgeois family of textile industrialists, based in Barmen, Germany. His family also owned a textile mill in Manchester, England, where F. Engels spent a large part of his life working as mill manager.

*The term 'Marxism' was unknown in Marx's lifetime. His comment, reported by Engels that "all I know is that I am not a Marxist," was made in reference to phrases used by his son-in-law Paul Lafargue.

Appendix B

'Philosophy or *'Poetry'*
A Critical Study of T. Watsuji's
Climate's Account

Introductory remarks

In 1993, I participated as a postgraduate foreign research student at the Graduate School of the University of Tokyo in a seminar about the Japanese 'philosopher' T. Watsuji (1889–1960). The professor in charge of this seminar Wataru Hiromatsu (1933–1994), had, after reading my report—this appendix—urged me to read it in the seminar. Unfortunately, professor W. Hiromatsu, who had a terminal disease, wasn't able to attend this seminar on 18 January 1994, but from the hospital he thanked me in writing for my contribution.

Recently, I was surprised to learn that this seminar about the 'philosopher' T. Watsuji will enter the next millenium. My friend H. Schiering's comment on my report and his criticism of T. Watsuji's ideas will clarify to anyone my surprise about the continuation of this seminar. Except for the opening and closing sentences, hereby H. Schiering's letter about my report *A Critical Study of T. Watsuji's Climate's Account:*

> *I don't have any real criticism regarding your formulations, on the contrary. What I'd like to add, that's my disposition, I think, is that without really maintaining respect you try to clarify from which point of view Mister [Watsuji] expresses his opinion. (For that matter, I think that his opinions are, to say the least, foolish, and on reflection too, I can't discover the meaning of his efforts; does he owe his popularity to his writing style? Setting down something beautifully in writing, can be enjoyed aesthetically, but doesn't say anything about the truth, does it?) If I understand it well, he connects the climate in which peole live with certain characterisations to which people conform to. As such, he considers man in so far as man like a huan being reacts on climate. Excellent, but then he goes ten streets too far.*

Your method of critizing is to my thinking 100% correct: to provide the counter-proof in concrete instances. It is interesting to consider what he then could answer. His theory doesn't provide any answer. His theory can be framed as follows: man is determined by his environment; the climate in which man grows up and in which he lives. Man is mainly a climatically determined being. This doesn't justify and explain:
- individual differences between people,
- exceptions to the rule,
- man's internal motives and inspiration,
- man's social involvement,
- tensions that might exist between—I—and—that which exists outside me—,
- (differences in degree of development of) consciousness. 'I understand this or that, and I act consequently.'
- dynamics in internal and external quantities. It's possible to reduce the issue to: man is hereditary determined or determined by his environment.
*Wrong questions are raised if one is open to the fact that dialectical interactions are occurring: man is determined by internal and external factors in a dynamical interaction; the issue doesn't become **or**, or **but**, and, **and**. What does the dynamic development look like with a person with these and those 'inclinations, talents' who finds himself or herself in situation A, B or C?*

*NB The advocates of the **or**, **or**-ideology generally withdraw in their safe-hide-out. This fits excellently in a conservative society, it gives self-affirmation of the old established values of the system.*

This letter doesn't need any additional comment, let's turn our attention to the report and it will become immediately clear why I was surprised that T. Watsuji's philosophy is still being studied.

Preface

According to T. Watsuji's philosophy; I, as a European, am a mixed product of meadow and desert types of climate, which makes me capable of moral passion, gentle love and, abstract and rational reasoning. These are nice qualities that T. Watsuji bestows on me. On the other hand, I don't feel honored at all to be in the same group with people such as A. Hitler and M. Heidegger.

In the preface of his book *Climate, (Fudo)*, written in the years 1928–1929 and published in 1935, T. Watsuji states the following purpose; 'to clarify the function of climate as a factor, within the structure of human existence.'

In this short essay I will occupy myself with the questions:

- How did T. Watsuji clarify the function of climate?

- What conclusions did T. Watsuji draw from his study?

As to my method of comment, I will review a number of quotations from the book *Climate*. I didn't take any quotations from the first chapter 'The Basic Principles of Climate', because it is merely a philosophical coating of T. Watsuji's motivation 'to put the problem of climatic characteristics under the searchlight of radical research.'

Chapter 4, 'Climate in Art' wasn't worthwile quoting either, since it presents an endless repetition of the basic thoughts from the preceding chapters.

In spite of going ahead of my conclusions, I am obliged to warn the reader that *Climate* isn't the work of a philosopher, or differently expressed, T. Watsuji doesn't show himself to be a philosopher by writing a fictional account about the function of climate!

Peasant Uprisings.

The distinctive character, then, of human nature in the monsoon zone can be understood as submissive and resignatory. It is the humidity that reveals this character.[1]

In drawing this conclusion, T. Watsuji ignored the long history of peasant uprisings in his own country. Thousands of farmers uprisings were registered during the Tokugawa period. In these uprisings, thousands of farmers, armed with bamboo spears, later on also with swords and guns, presented their complaints in petition to the local lord. When their demands were refused, which happened quite often, the farmers would smash the homes of the wealthy men in their district.

Also, Watsuji didn't consider the uprisings and revolutions that have taken place in India, Indonesia and China, although these countries are in the monsoon zone. T. Watsuji's conclusion about a submissive and resignatory human nature in the monsoon zone sounds pretentiously false.

Java: no culture

This factor (a straightforward summer) helps us to understand why the people of the South Seas have never made any appreciable cultural progress. The climate of the South Seas affords man a rich supply of food; hence his attitude is that all is well as long as he is blessed with nature's generosity.

…There is no incentive to stimulate the development of productive capacity. Hence, apart the rare occasion when huge Buddhist pagodas were built in Java under the spur of Indian culture, the people of the South Seas have given birth to no cultural monuments [correct translation ought to be: given birth to no culture]. *So they became easy prey for and ready lackeys of the Europeans after the Renaissance.* [3]

In the foregoing quoted passage, T. Watsuji clarifies the function of climate as failing to stimulate the productive capacity which in turn he links to the absence of culture. 'All year round a single type of season' clarifies for T. Watsuji the function of climate as a factor within the structure of human existence in the South Seas. First I will quote a good definition of the term culture: 'Culture expresses itself in the knowledge, beliefs, art, morals, law and all other capacities and habits acquired by man as a member of society.' [4] Did T. watsuji acquaint himself with all these aspects of culture in the South Seas? His writing doesn't show any results—in this way—of scholarly, painstakingly investigating historical and sociocultural sources. Ranking cultures into superior or inferior ones, exisiting or non-existing ones, falls outside the scope of this essay. I think it more appropriate to speak about cultures in progression and cultures in regression.

The culture of Java was in regression because of four hundred years of Dutch colonisation. When T. Watsuji noticed that there was no incentive to stimulate the development of productive capacity, he should have asked himself the questions; How did it come about that four hundred years ago, the Dutch East India Company, the VOC, had such a strong interest in Java? Why was it that the Dutch made Java their stronghold of colonial trade? If T. Watsuji would have looked around in Amsterdam, he might have seen to what the people of Java have given birth.

No escape for India's people

Over two-thirds of India's 320 millions (a fifth of the world's population) are farmers and grow their crops thanks to the monsoon. In general, apart from the few areas where there is a plentiful supply of water, the food of the household and the fodder of the animals depend on the monsoon; whether it is late, whether it lasts its due time and brings its due amount of rain are matters of great moment. If the monsoon is abnormal, then a bad crop ensues, bad enough to bring calamity. Anciently there were famines whenever such bad years occured. In recent times, with modern transport facilities, such famines can be forstalled. But there is no remedy for the hardships of India's farmers......Even today there is no means of resistance against nature, no escape for India's people from such insecurity of life. [5]

Complete dependency on the monsoon and no resistance against nature are deplorable arguments. If capital resources and expertise are available, farmers might have a good grip on—the influences of—nature. People can build dykes and greenhouses. They can dig wells and install sprinklers to provide water in times of drought. They can plant trees to hold the soil in place and foliage makes a windbreak and conserves moisture. All these means of nature control were, at the beginning of this century, already in widespread use in Western Europe. Beyond my own observation, Gunmar Myrdal recognizes likewise the grip—to a certain degree—which man in South Asia may have on his natural environment.

> *Soils can be enriched, animals and people better housed, health measures vastly improved, refrigeration and air conditioning more widely applied, erosion losses reduced, buildings and equipment better adopted to withstand excessive heat and humidity, insects more effectively controlled, and so on. But these are costly investments that imply a level of economic achievement substantially greater than at present and compete with many other pressing demands that may be deemed essential for economic growth.* [6]

Evidently, there are means of resistance against nature—possibilities for the Indian people to escape from 'such' insecurity in life.

The climatic path or the proletarian revolution

It is on such grounds (the Indian as a symbol from oppression) that the visitor to India is made to wish impulsively that the Indian would take up his struggle for independence. In this sense, although his cotton may well glut the world's markets, the Indian is receptive and resigned as ever; witness his policy of non-resistance and passive obedience. The physical strength of the Indian laborer is said to be far less even than that of the Chinese, and no more than a quarter or a third of that of his Western counterpart; but neither this, nor his distinctive nature can be transformed overnight.

For this distinctive nature has been moulded by climate, and change depends upon the conquest of climate. This latter can only be achieved by a climatic path—by the attainment historically, of an awareness of climate. This done, man may surmount climate. [7]

Contrary to T. Watsuji's solution of transforming the Indian's physical strength and distinctive nature by the climatic path, one of my solutions would be increasing the Indians' calorie and protein intake. See the Table on the next page. This Table shows us that the average person in South Asia does not receive adequate nutrition. Estimated minimumdaily calorie requirements are 2,000 to 2,300 with an estimated minimum daily protein requirement of 65 grammes a day for each adult. In 1958, the United States daily calorie was 3,100 for each person, with a daily protein intake of 91 grammes for each person. South Asian daily calorie and protein intake statistics for pre-war times were the same or even worse. G. Myrdal specifies: 'Comparisons with pre-war times…suggest that by 1958 the calorie supply slightly surpassed the 1934–1938 level in the Philippines and the Indian subcontinent but was about the same or little lower elsewhere.' [8]

Development or underdevelopment. Starting from the supposition that 'climate' didn't undergo remarkable changes from before the Colonial Era till 1960, then it stands out that the pictures of food supply-fluctuation in relation to population growth, aren't so different for Europe as for South Asia. 'In the pre-industrial era, Western Europeans seem generally to have been fairly well fed between famines, and it is perhaps not unreasonable to assume that the same was true of South Asians. It is probable, though, that in both regions some population groups were chronically short of food.'[9]

Calorie and protein content of post-war food supplies[10]

Calorie and protein content of post-war food supplies

Country and year		Total	Deficit of Requirements (%)	percent accounted for by:		Proteins (g)
				Cereals	Animal Products	
Pakistan	1949-50	1,010	- 8.9	78	9	48
	1951-53	2,000	-11.2	75	9	46
	1954-56	1,990	-11.6	74	9	47
	1957-59	1,980	-12.0	76	8	46
	1960-61*	1,970	-12.4	78	8	45
India	1949-50	1,630	-29.1	70	7	44
	1951-53	1,700	-26.1	70	7	46
	1954-56	1,840	-20.0	67	7	49
	1957-59	1,900	-17.4	67	6	51
	1960-61*	1,990	-13.5	68	6	53
Philippines	1952-53*	1,790	-18.3	68	7	46
	1957-59	1,870	-15.5	67	10	47
	1960*	1,950	-11.4	65	9	51
Ceylon	1952-53	1,990	-13.1	58	4	43
	1954-56	2,070	- 9.6	59	4	44
	1957-59	2,030	-11.4	61	5	45
	1961*	2,060	-10.0	60	4	44

Sources : U.N., Statistical Year book 1962, Table 128, pp. 330-332; U.N.,Compedium of Social Satistics: 1963, Table 18., 163; and Fod and Agroculture Organization, Production Yearbook, vol.16, 1962, Rome, Table 96B pp. 251-252
*Tentative data

Under the same climatic circumstances, Asia was, in the pre-colonial period, independent and on an equal footing with Europe. A. G. Frank notes about this period that: 'Asia, in general sold its agricultural and manufactured products to European traders who called and/or established themselves on coastal enclaves and paid in gold and silver. Europe had little else to offer civilised Asians and still lacked or could not finance sufficient military power to enforce trade or production on them. [11]

Since T. Watsuji didn't provide any explanation about the causes of the development of underdevelopment in India, let us try to fill this gap. According to E. Mandel[a]: 'caused the penetration of money econmy into the agricultural economy of Western Europe a considerable expansion of the commodities production, and created in this way the condition for the birth of industrial capitalism...Well then, nowhere outside Europe could the agricultural surplus product take up the everlasting form of money-interest.' [12] In India there were no important qualitative changes in the mode of production during the first stage of world capitalist development (1500–1700). The rent of land was still being paid for by agricultural products.

In the same analysis E. Mandel observes that the accumulation of capital in Western Europe, from the tenth till the eighteenth century got concentrated into the hands of the bourgeoisie who gradually liberated themselves from the custody of the feudal classes and state, and made the state an instrument to accelerate the process of capital accumulation for its own advantage.

> *On the other hand, in the other pre-capitalist civilizations capital remained continuously subjected to the arbitrariness of a despotic and all mighty state....Except for Japan, where from the fourteenth century, the pirate merchants infested the Chinese and Philippine Seas and accumulated a considerable amount of capital. This accumulation happened at the same time while the authority of the state faded away and the bank-merchantsmen had superiority over the nobility and from then the development of manufacture capital, made a repetition of the capitalistic development of Western Europe possible with a delay of two hundred years and independent of this.* [13]

How much did India and the other colonies contribute to the process and concentration of capital accumulation in Europe? E. Mandel estimates the amount to be over a billion pounds sterling for the period of 1500–1750. For the period of 1760–1815, E. Mandel concludes that 'the profits from the West Indies and India alone, more than doubled the accumulation of money available for the rising industry in Great Britain.' [14] The total British plunder of India for the period between 1752–1815 is estimated at £1000 million.

Here, I will add a brief description about the mechanisms of European capital accumulation at the expense of the colonies, especially valid for the period 1500–1770. European traders plundered the Americas for gold and silver, looted the East Indies (spices), enslaved Africans etc., which we may call primitive methods of capital accumulation. Another method was, for example, paying for India's agricultural and manufactured products with stolen or cheaply produced silver.

Market exchange forces also worked to the advantage of the European metropolis as Karl Marx observed:

> *Capital invested in foreign trade can yield a higher rate of profit, firstly, because it competes with commodities produced by other countries with less developed production facilities, so that the more advanced country sells its goods above their value, even though still more cheaply than its competitors... The priviliged country recovers more labour in exchange for less, even though this difference, the excess, is pocketed by a particular class, just as in the exchange between labour and capital in general.* [15]

---

[a] Ernest Mandel (1923–1994), widely acknowledged as the foremost Marxist economist, editor, occupied leading positions in the Socialist Workers Party and the Fourth International.

Destruction of India's mode of production. While India's mode of production hadn't undergone significant changes so far, from the second period of colonisation (1770–1870), the process of underdevelopment, de-industrialisation and de-urbanisation of India's industrial economy took on definite forms. British industrial traders imposed duties on imports that were five to twenty times as high as permitted. Through these measures India's textile industry, and similarly its iron and steel industries, were destroyed. This destruction was being reinforced by the export of British manufactured goods to India.

Marx explains: 'In so far as English trade has had a revolutionary effect on the mode of production in India, this is simply to the extent that it has destroyed spinning and weaving, which form an age-old and integral part of this unity of industrial and agricultural production, through the low price of English commodities. In this way it has torn the community to pieces.' [16]

Thus the previously highly developed village artisantry had to be absorbed again into village agriculture. But here, British rule had transformed the zamindari latifundia[b] by introduction of many layers of renters, usurers and tax collectors into a system dependent on capitalism. A. G. Frank concludes: 'The growing need for raw materials and foodstuffs then converted the South of the Indian subcontinent into a plantation enonomy not dissimilar to the Latin American ones.' [17]

British rule: cause of India's problems. For the imperialist period (1870–1930) and afterwards, we may state that India exemplifies all the major structural factors in the capitalist development of underdevelopment. A large drain of economic surplus to the metropolis took place during this period. To continue this drain, the British used the construction of the Indian railroad and the national debt. These railroads were used to get raw materials out of India and bring manufactured commodities in. Railway construction cost was added to the Indian debt, which was in its turn an instrument 'for extracting the economic surplus from the colony to the metropolis.'[18]

The drain of India's economic surplus continues taking place through unequal import-export exchange: India's main exports are raw materials (tea, jute, raw cotton) and her main imports are steel, machinery, transport equipment and textiles.

Another major obstacle for India's development was the growth of quisling classes whose interests have been tied to the development of the metropolis and to the underdevelopment of its own economy. The writer J. Nehru wrote the following summarizing account of India's problems:

> *Nearly all our major problems today have grown up during British rule and as a direct result of British policy: the princes; the minority problem; various vested interests, foreign and Indian; the lack of industry and the neglect of agriculture; the extreme backwardness in the social services; and above all, the tragic poverty of the people.'* [19]

---

[b] Zamindari latifundia refers to India's estate system of landholding and revenue collection in kinds (goods or natural produce) by zamindars (collectors). Under Muslim rule, the revenues were collected for the Indian government, under British rule this system changed into a feudatory, having rights of private property in a large amount of land by paying to the government a fixed substantial revenue raised from the cultivators.

Some measures to help India's development. From the foregoing I conclude that the climate factor didn't play an influential role in the process of the development of India's underdevelopment. Factors such as colonisation, destruction of India's mode of production, unequal exchange of import-export products, a class of Indian quislings etc. have played and are playing a decisive role 'in moulding the Indian's distinctive nature' (T. Watsuji).

Solving India's problems by taking a 'climatic path' seems to me rather odd. The path of political independence didn't produce great results either. India was and continues to be one of the poorest countries in the world, struggling with hunger, malnutrition and unemployment. Instead of the 'climatic path' I would like to suggest some different measures that might help India's development.

1. A 'communist' revolution to abolish the very unhealthy situation in which one percent of the population gets fifty percent of the national income.

2. An economically independent policy towards the further advanced nations such as the U.S.A., Europe and Japan, and her multinationals. Quisling power must be destroyed to acquire a stronger trading position.

3. Improvement of agricultural productivity and accelerating planned industrialisation carried out by the Indian people themselves.

No weed-grass in Europe

Then professor Otsuki said something quite astonishing: 'There is no weed-grass in Europe, you know.' This was something very near to a revelation to me; and it was at the point that I began to grasp what it is that distinguishes Europe's climate.

I can assure professor Otsuki and T. Watsuji that removing weed-grass is one of the most labor intensive activities in European agriculture. So, it's nonsense to deny the existence of weed-grass in Europe.

Unity under the Italian sun

So Rome's predilection for unity must be understood in the context of Italy's climate. Civitas Romana was a true child of Italy, unrelated to the Greek polis. Then, as a later expression of Rome's unifying power, came the Catholic Church, a universal and unifying church that was to dominate Europe for more than a thousand years. [21]

'I will briefly comment on this 'unifying' church. The Catholic Church was the counterpart of feudalism in Mediaeval Europe: it harmed and obstructed society's political and social progress. Apart from the—outside—society, how did this 'unification' mechanism work inside the church? From the eleventh century protests from within the church were voiced. Known are the doctrines of a group of Christians[22] that had occupied the castle of Montforte in the Italian diocese Asti, who, alas were condemned to the flames. In Rome itself, Arnold Brescia had revolted against the church in 1145. Part of the discipline of the Holy St. Franciscus, founded in the Italian city Assasi, separated and formed their discipline of the Fraticelli. They expected and preached the coming era of the Holy Spirit. The Fraticellis were strongly opposed to the wealth and hierarchy of the Catholic Church. The Church understood their grave threat and extinguished all of them by sword and fire. Well, what a predilection for unity under the Italian sun—not to mention the tardy process of Italy's unification.

Unbearable heat and flat roofs in Japan

Man [in Europe] *can build his house making no provision against unbearable heat or humidity and concerning himself only with the cold atmosphere. There is no need to provide against a stagnant and immobile humidity by means of the continual circulation of air as in Japan; thus the warmed air is separated from the world outside by thick, dry walls and remains in the room a long time before it is emitted artificially. A cold atmosphere, then, is much more readily overcome than a heat combined with humidity. Nor do the provisions for retaining the heat need to be more than elementary; I doubt whether, in fact, much more heating fuel is used in England and France than in Japan.*'[23]

I will give some numbers that provide a general indication of the differences in temperature and humidity between Europe and Japan.

	Latitude	Average Yearly Temperature	Average Yearly Degree of Humidity
Akita	(N 40)	11.8 C	73%
Marseilles	(N 43)	14.4 C	69%
Wakkanai	(N 46)	7.3 C	76%
Paris	(N 46)	10.5 C	79%
Tokyo	(N 37)	16.4 C	64%
Athenes	(N 38)	17.7 C	62%

Adapted from Yomiuri Nenkan Data File, 1933; numbers for Akita and Wakkanai are given for the year 1991. The numbers for Marseilles, Paris, Tokyo and Athenes are based on the period from 1951–1980.

These figures clearly show that the European ought to concern himself, too, with unbearable heat and humidity. Over centuries it has been customary to cover the top of a house with a sloping roof. This type of roof protects against heat and is very efficient getting rid of heavy rainfall. Sloping roofs are still most common in Europe, while nowadays in Japan municipial flats are topped with only flat roofs. Can using the inferior flat roof in Japan be caused by some unknown climatic factor? 'Nor do provisions for retaining the heat need to be more than elementary,' is an odd remark considering the double walls and double glass windows used in my home country.

T. Watsuji's Poetry

[about the summer in Western Europe] *Because of humidity in the atmosphere and the consequent insignificance of day and night temperature variation one can walk in the meadows early in the morning and not wet one's feet; for the same reason, the farmer can leave his tools in the fields when he goes home at night. This is something quite unusual for Japanese eyes, accustomed as they are to seeing the Japanese farmer carrying his spade or his hoe home from his paddy, washing off the mud and putting them away in his shed. It is probably quite beyond the imagination of the Japanese that one could leave tools in the field all night without their becoming rusted...I walked in the Grünewald and the Thüringian forest near Weimar looking deliberatedly for insects but the wooded parts here, where there was hardly any grass underneath the trees, did not produce even a single ant. All I did see was a flight of moths, all of the same kind, winging their way in the same direction. This was barely credible at first to one accustomed to watching the illimitable variety of insects on a Japanese hill in the summer. But Japan's insects, next to her typhoons, her floods and her droughts, menace her crops. Western Europe, by contrast, is like heaven on earth.* [24]

I don't mind if T. Watsuji likes to write poetry, likes to line up words for beauty's sake, but as a philosopher, he shouldn't tell lies. I will rely on my own Western European agricultural background to refute the foregoing passage. Occasionally there is no dew on the fields in the morning, but more often there is dew. During harvest time, famers often have to wear water-resistant clothes, especially between five and nine in the morning. The fields, very wet and cold because of the dew, aren't an invitation to take a walk. European farmers leaving their tools in the fields might occasionally happen but in my home district (the southern part of Holland), it is an exception to the rule.

Probably T. Watsuji didn't grow up on a farm, or he had known that washing a spade makes it even rustier. These tools have to be brushed off and 'oiled', if you want to protect them from rusting away. Although there is a difference in degree of humidity between Europe and Japan, the fact remains that tools left behind in the fields rust away as easily in Europe as in Japan. But this rusting also depends on the quality of the tools.

Why T. Watsuji deliberatedly looked for insects in the Grünewald woods puzzles me. The threat from the European woods lies in the existence of rabbits, hares, deer, wolves, birds etc. Fences around the fields have to be in perfect condition or a complete crop might be eaten away by these denizens of the woods. It's even harder to stop flocks of birds from destroying harvests, which regularly happens. Western Europe isn't like 'heaven on earth'; I remember storms hailstorms that destroyed complete harvests, sometimes including greenhouses. I remember the great bursts of the Dutch dykes when thousands of people and cattle died. However, as the proverb goes that God created the earth but the Dutch people Holland; I believe in the overall control of climate by sensible man.

Japan's mountain zones

…there is hardly any land in western Europe that is not put to some use. The case with Japan is very different where a large proportion of the land is mountainous and not very readily directed by man. It would be wrong to claim that such mountain zones are entirely without utility; yet, even supposing that lumber for export purposes were required from Japan's mountains, production facilities are far from adequate in that the precipitous nature of the slopes makes transportation a complex problem. Further, afforestation in Japan is no simple matter, there being many tree varieties good for nothing but use as fuel.[25]

It's no wonder that a large proportion of the mountainous land in Japan isn't 'readily directed' by man when there were always rigid prohibitions in effect against the farmers using 'their' forests. The Japanese novelist Shimazaki Toson (1872–1943), gives a good account about the 'use' of forests in Japan:

> *The five trees of the Kiso were the hinoki, sawara, asuhi, koya maki, and nezuko, all evergreens. The mountains around had been divided by the Shogunate [c] and by*

Owari ^d into nesting forests where hawks for the use of the imperial court and the

Owari ᵈ into nesting forests where hawks for the use of the imperial court and the shogunate nested, closed forests and open forests. The nesting forests and the closed forests were strictly forbidden to the villagers. Even in the open forests, the only ones that were freely accessible, it was forbidden to cut any of the five trees without special permission. This had been done to preserve the forests. The fine timber produced in this region was important to Owari, and the rules were rigorously enforced. [26]

From historical viewpoint we may say that factors such as climate or the degree of steepness, didn't play a deciding role in determining the fate of Japan's mountain zones.

Gloomy thoughts

Abstraction is a valuable ability, one offered to Germany's philosophers by the gloom of western Europe. Their climate denied this talent to the philosophers of the ancient world.[27]

Despite the bright climate in their countries the Greek philosopher Plato, the Chinese philosopher Mengtse formulated **abstract** theories about commodity and monetary production. Or how about the philosopher Abd-al-Rahman ibn Khaldoen (1332–1402), who in the Islamic Empire, precised political-econmic ideas and fit these ideas into a philosophy that approached historical materialism (four hundred and fifty years before K. Marx).

On the other hand, T. Watsuji forgot to explain climate's **gloomy** influence upon his contemporary philosopher M Heidegger. In T. Watsuji's phrasing it would could be formulated like this: Fascist sympathies are an expression of climatic based disposition, one offered to Germany's philosophers by the gloom of Western Europe. After his acceptance of the rectorship at the University of Freiburg, M. Heidegger made public appeals to support his Führer A. Hitler. Hereby one of M. Heidegger's gloomy appeals:

German students (November 3, 1933)
The National Socialist revolution is bringing about the total transformation of our German existence [Dasein]…The Führer alone is the present and future German reality and its law. Learn to know ever more deeply; from now on every single thing demands decision, and every action responsibility.
Heil Hitler!
Martin Heidegger, Rector [28]

This gloomy-depressive quotation needs no further comment.

---

[c] Shogunate: the office of a military governor of Japan before the mid 19th century with power exceeding the emperor's.

[d] Owari: an area-roughly corresponding to modern Aichi prefecture—controlled by a feudal lord.

T. Watsuji's objectivity

The Thirty Years War in Germany...Even girls played a part in this battle. Until I went to Rothenburg, I had never thought of war in such terms; it should have been fought only by those with combatant qualifications, either as conscripts or by their own choice. This was how wars were fought in Japan, even in 'Age of War' in the fifteenth and sixteenth centuries. To the best of my knowledge, there has never once been a war in Japan in which children helped in the defence of a town or a village. So I realised for the first time how destructive that war proved and was able to judge why the German population was reduced to a quarter. Thus western Europe's gloom reveals itself once more in war, for the impression of dark barbarism here is common with that given by mediaeval weapons. [29]

That mediaeval Europe was the stage of many barbarian wars and revolts isn't a point of dispute. What testifies against T. Watsuji's objectivity is his silence about the barbarian side of civil wars and uprisings in Japan. In 1612 the Tokugawa government got alarmed by the political and military implications that were caused by the spread of Christianity. The Christian religion was prohibited, most of the foreign missionaries were murdered and almost three hundred thousand Christians were arrested. Standard methods employed by the Chief Commissioner of Nagasaki to obtain information or recantations from Christian prisoners included: 'the water torture, the ordeal of the snake pit, branding on the face, slicing with a bamboo saw, the torture of the wooden horse..., roasting alive, and (one of the imports from the West that the authorities accepted with undiluted enthusiasm) crucifixion.'[30]

Instead of considering 'terms' of war; how about the 'terms' of tax collection in Japan? In times of economic hardships, farmers often couldn't pay their taxes in time. The tax-collecting authorities, harassed the tax-defaulters with barbarian methods such as dressing people in a rough straw coat and then setting them on fire. When this method failed to produce the tax-payment, wives or daughters of the tax-defaulters were arrested and subjected to painful and humilating ordeals. Duarte Correa recounts the following outrage that took place in Shimabara:

> The daughter of a village headman was seized; and young and beautiful as she was, they exposed her nude and branded her all over the body with red-hot irons. The father, supposing that his girl would simply be kept as a hostage until his debt was paid, had accepted the separation; but, when he heard about the barbarous treatment to which she had been subjected, he became mad with grief and, summoning his friends, attacked the local bailiff and killed him. [30]

What was the fate of Japanese children and women in times of civil war? In the Shimabara revolt (1637–1638), about forty thousand men, women and children fortified themselves in Hara Castle. The Shogunal forces' began their all out-attack against this castle on 12 April and two days later, 'The attackers systemetically set fire to the huts and trenches, [of Hara Castle] and [its] occupants were burnt to death by the hundreds, others including large numbers of women with their children, hurled themselves into the flames rather than be taken alive.' [32]

Conclusion; T. Watsuji's objectivity leaves much to be desired.

The separability of history and climate

History and climate act as the shield and buckler of culture; the two are quite inseparable, for there is no historical event that does not possess its climatic character, nor is there climatic phenomenon that is without its historical component. So, if we can discover climate within a historical event, then we can also read history within climatic phenomena. All that I have attempted to do is to examine these two factors, while restricting my attention primarily to climate. [33]

The history of humankind as well as that of other living species; starts from the primacy of material survival. Unlike all other species, humankind produces means of subsistence and reproduction, through deliberate and collective action: social labour. Climatic factors play an important role in the early development of the production that provides humankind with its necessary products for survival. But factors, such as division of labor, accumulation of a constant social surplus product, increase of knowledge and productivity of labor and social-political structures have grown away from climate.

Instead of the climatic component within a historical event, I attach more importance to the struggle component: 'Men and women make their own history. They do not make it free from any material constraints, within an unlimited range of possibilities. But they do make it, and the concrete historical process depends in the first place on the outcome of their struggles.' [34]

Inside the house no distinction?

> *It will be readily acknowledged that the family system has no longer the prominence or power that it possessed in Tokugawa days...it could not on any account argued that the Japanese, in spite of the adoption of capitalism, ceased to see the individual in the house. To cite the most everyday phenomenon, the Japanese understand the house as 'inside' and the world beyond as 'outside'. Within this 'inside', all distinction between individuals disappear...Thus the 'house', or the 'inside' is regarded as the family as a whole, a relationship admitting no discrimination, but very strictly segregated from the 'outside' world.* [35]

Especially before adopting capitalism in Japan, the individual in the house was non-existent. The Japanese family has been a unit, sharing social and economic responsibility for over centuries. In the Tokugawa period, not the individual but the 'house' owned property. Succession through adoption exemplifies this shared economic responsibility.

> *In Japan the crucial question often was the suitability for the succession; even a natural son might be bypassed if considered lacking in the necessary qualities. A fairly common solution for households with unsuitable sons, or no sons at all, was to adopt a son-in-law, or even to adopt a young girl and then choose for her a suitable husband who could subsequently be adopted into the household.* [36]

When natural children are by passed in the matter of succession, can the family be described as 'a relationship admitting no discrimination?'

Public landownership in a slave society

The Taika Reformation [seventh century] achieved a social structure of national socialism based on the principle of public land ownership; and even such drastic reform could be effected without even the smallest civil disturbance because of the religious authority that lay behind economic power. [37]

The law of Taika (Great Change) 'based on the principle of public landowner-ship', was enacted upon the Statutes of Taiho in a society where the people were divided into citizens and 'slaves'. How did this land reform affect the lives of the new class of 'public land owners', or more precisely expressed, the oppressed peasants?

> *Before the Taiho statute was enacted all the peasants were put upon, oppressed and hardly* [sic] *driven, and after the Taiho statute they were driven equally hard to feed the governing class. Before the Taiho statute the levies of labour and products on the peasants were irregular and variable, but after Taiho the imposition of labour and products became regular and rates were fixed.* [38]

A society in which peasants lead a slave-like existence, are subjected to land tax, poll-tax and compulsory labor, and where a small ruling class leads a parasitic life, has nothing whatsoever in common with national socialism. Moreover, in those days Japan wasn't a nation yet.

Motive power behind Meiji Restoration (1867)

Reverence for the Emperor, the symbol of unity of the religious grouping, was indeed the motive power behind the Meiji Restoration. Feudal princes attempting to resist this by military power alone could achieve no division among the forces working for the Restoration and they disintegrated eventually in the face of the nation as a whole. [39]

According to various sources, 'reverence for the Emperor' wasn't the motive power behind the Meiji Restoration.

> *It was neither the doctrine of the divine right of the Mikado nor the doctrine of the exclusion of foreigners that had really brought about the great change: the chief cause of the downfall of the Shogunate lay in the economic condition of the country, which had outgrown the feudal government.* [40]

> *The real objective, in fact was not to restore power to the person of the sovereign (in 1867 Emperor Meiji was a youth of fifteen who was hardly in a position to assert his country's prestige in the world) or even to the Imperial Family and court nobility, but to bring about certain reforms that seemed urgently necessary if Japan was to avoid the fate inflicted by Western powers on India and, more recently, on China.* [41]

I offer no opinion on the motive power behind the Meiji Restoration; though I reject T. Watsuji's oversimplified comments on this subject.

Conclusions

A philosopher ought to be in quest of wisdom, knowledge and truth. In research; opinions, impressions, guesses have to be verified and replaced by knowledge.

What did we observe about T. Watsuji's observations and comments?

1. T. Watsuji draws the wrong conclusion about the submissive and resignatory—human nature in the monsoon zone.

2. T. Watsuji doesn't understand the term culture.

3. T. Watsuji uses deplorable arguments, such as complete dependency on the monsoon and no means of resistance against nature, in describing the fate of India's people.

4. T. Watsuji's solution of taking the climatic path for solving India's problems, is a rather odd way.

5. T. Watsuji makes makes nonsensical remarks about the non-existence of weed-grass in Europe.

6. T. Watsuji doesn't get the picture of the provisions that are necessary for retaining the heat in Europe.

7. T. Watsuji likes to write poems, expressing his noble thoughts about agriculture, weather, insects and farmer's tools in Europe. However this poetry is alienated from European reality.

8. By his inadequate explanation of the 'development' of Japan's mountain zones, T. Watsuji shows that he doesn't have any economic-political insights about the developments in his own country.

9. T. Watsuji can't see the wrong side of climate's gloomy influence, as in the case of his contemporary philosopher M. Heidegger.

10. T. Watsuji's silence about the barbarian side of civil wars and uprisings in Japan, testifies against his objectivity.

11. T. Watsuji is ignorant[c] of the struggle component within historical events.

The overall balance sheet indicates that T. Watsuji might be a poet but surely isn't worthy to be considered a philosopher.

---

[e] This ignorance also manifests itself in T. Watsuji's mechanical interpretation of Marxism—ignoring the humanistic and revolutionary aspects of Marxism—in his book 'Ethics as Anthropology'.

NOTES

1. Watsuji Tetsuro, *A Climate* (*Fudo*), translated by G. Bownas, Printing Bureau, Japanese Government, 1962, p. 20.

2. H. Borton, *Peasant Uprisings in Japan*, 1968, New York

3. W. Tetsuro, *A Climate*, p. 22.

4. Claude Lévi-Strauss, *Interviews*, Chicago and London, The University of Chicago Press, 1991, p. 165.

5. T. Watsuji, *Climate*, p. 25.

6. Gunmar Myrdal, *Asian Drama*, New York, Pantheon, 1967, p. 2138.

7. T. Watsuji, 'Climate', p. 38.

8. Gunmar Myrdal, *Asian Drama*, New York, Pantheon, 1967. p. 547.

9. Ibid., p. 1556.

10. Ibid., Vol. 1.

11. Andre Gunder Frank, *Dependent Accumulation and Underdevelopment*, London and Basingstoke, The MacMillan Press Ltd., 1978, pp. 17-18.

12. Ernest Mandel, *De economische theorie van het marxisme*, original title *Traité d'économie marxiste*, Holland, Bussum, Dutch translation, Het Wereldvenster, 1980, English translation by W. P. M. Nuyten.

13. Ibid., pp. 120-121.

14. Andre Gunder Frank, *Dependent Accumulation*, p. 73.

15. Karl Marx, *Capital* Volume 3, London, Penguin Books Ltd., 1991, pp. 344-345.

16. Ibid., pp. 451-452.

17. Andre Gunder Frank, *Dependent Accumulation*, p. 90.

18. Ibid., p. 147.

19. Ibid., p. 148.

20. T. Watsuji, *Climate*, p. 60.

21. Ibid., p. 97.

22. H. P. G. Quack, *De socialisten*, Holland, Baarn, Het Wereldvenster, 1977, Volume 1, p. 70, English transla tion by W. P. M. Nuyten.

23. T. Watsuji, *Climate*, p. 100.

24. Ibid., pp. 102-103.

25. Ibid., p. 107.

26. Toson Shimazaki, *Before The Dawn*, original title 'Yo-ake Mae', translated by William E. Naff, Honolulu, University of Hawaii Press, 1987, p. 11.

27. T. Watsuji, *Climate*, p. 112.

28. Richard Wollin, *The Heidegger Controversy*, Massachusetts, Cambridge, The MIT Press, 1993, pp. 46-47.

29. T. Watsuji, *Climate*, p. 116.

30. Ivan Morris, The Nobility of Failure, Tokyo, Charles E. Tuttle Company, Inc. 1982, p. 148.

31. Ibid., p. 152.

32. Ibid., p. 171.

33. T. Watsuji, *Climate*, pp. 116-117.

34. Ernest Mandel, *The Place of Marxism in History*, New Jersey, Humanities Press, 1994, p. 11.

35. T. Watsuji, *Climate*, p. 144.

36. Karel van Wolferen, *The Enigma of Japanese Power*, London MacMillan London Limited, 1989, p. 165.

37. T. Watsuji, *Climate*, p. 154.

38. Yosoburo Takekoshi, *The Economic Aspects of the History of of the Civilization of Japan*, London, George Allen &Unwin Ltd., 1930p. 33.

39. W. Tetsuro, *Climate*, p. 155.

40. Matsuyo Takizawa, *The Penetration of Money Economy in Japan*, New York, Colombia University Press, 1927, p. 143.

41. Ivan Morris, *The Nobility of Failure*, Tokyo, Charles E. Tuttle Company, Inc. 1982, p. 240.

978-0-595-40379-0
0-595-40379-4

www.ingramcontent.com/pod-product-compliance
Lightning Source LLC
Chambersburg PA
CBHW020418290526
45785CB00002B/618